William Shakespeare

Julius Caesar

Edited by

Maurice Charney

with a Theatre Commentary by

Stuart Vaughan

Other Titles in the Applause Shakespeare Library:

King Lear
Macbeth
A Midsummer Night's Dream
The Tempest

Table of Contents

The Applause Shakespeare Library
Julius Caesar

Edited by Maurice Charney
Commentary by Stuart Vaughan
General Series Editor: John Russell Brown

Library of Congress Cataloging-in-Publication Data
Shakespeare, William, 1564-1616
Julius Caesar / William Shakespeare ; edited by Maurice Charney and Stuart Vaughan.
p. cm. — (The Applause Shakespeare Library)
Includes bibliographical references.
ISBN 1-55783-183-1 : $7.95
1. Caesar, Julius—Drama. 2. Rome—History—Civil War, 43-31 B.C. —Drama. 3. Rome—History—53-44 B.C. —Drama I. Charney, Maurice. II. Vaughan, Stuart. III. Title IV. Series
PR2808.A2C55 1994
822.3'3—dc20 94-30094
CIP

British Library Cataloging-in-Publication Data
A catalog record for this book is available from the British Library.

APPLAUSE BOOKS

211 West 71st Street
New York, NY 10023
Phone (212) 496-7511
Fax: (212) 721-2856

406 Vale Road
Tonbridge Kent TN9 1XR
Phone 073 235-7755
Fax 073 207-7219

General Preface to the Applause Shakespeare Library

This edition is designed to help readers see and hear the plays in action. It gives an impression of how actors can bring life to the text and shows how certain speeches, movements, or silences take on huge importance once the words have left the page and become part of a performance. It is a theatrical edition, like no other available at this time.

Everyone knows that Shakespeare wrote for performance and not for solitary readers or students in classrooms. Yet the great problem of how to publish the plays so that readers can understand their theatrical life is only beginning to be tackled. Various solutions have been tried. The easiest—and it is an uneasy compromise—is to commission some director or leading actor to write a preface about the play in performance and print that at the beginning of the volume, followed by a critical and historical introduction, the text and notes about verbal difficulties, a textual introduction, and a collation of variant readings as in any other edition. Another easy answer is to supply extensive stage directions to sort out how characters enter or exit and describe any gestures or actions that the text explicitly requires. Both methods give the reader little or no help in realizing the play in performance, moment by moment, as the text is read.

A more thorough-going method is to include some notes about staging and acting among the annotations of meaning, topical references, classical allusions, textual problems, and so forth. The snag here is that the theatrical details make no consecutive sense and cannot deal with the larger issues of the build-up of conflict or atmosphere, the developing impression of character, or the effect of group and individual movement on stage. Such notes offer, at best, intermittent assistance.

In the more expensive one-volume editions, with larger-than-usual formats, yet another method is used—to include a stage history of the play showing how other ages have staged the play and describing a few recent productions that have been more than usually successful with the critics. The snag here is that unavailable historical knowledge is required to interpret records of earlier performances. Moreover, the journalistic accounts of productions which are quoted in these histories are liable to emphasize what is unusual in a production rather than the opportunities offered to actors in any production of the play, the text's enduring theatrical vitality. In any case, all this material is kept separate from the rest of the book and not easily consulted during a reading of the text.

The Applause Shakespeare goes further than any of these. It does the usual tasks expected of a responsible, modern edition, but adds a very special feature: a continuous commentary on the text by a professional director or a leading actor that considers the stage life of the play as its action unfolds. It shows what is demanded from the actors—line by line where necessary—and points out what decisions about interpretation have to be made and the consequences of one choice over another. It indicates where emotional climaxes are placed—and where conflicting thoughts in the character's mind create subtextual pressures beneath the words. Visual statements are noted: the effect of groups of figures on stage, of an isolated figure, or of a pair of linked figures in a changing relationship; the effect of delayed or unexpected entries, sudden departures, slow or processional exeunts, or a momentarily empty stage. Everything that happens on stage comes within the notice of this commentary. A reader can "feel" what the play would be like in action.

What the commentary does not do is equally important from the reader's point of view. It does not try to provide a single theatrical reading of the text. Rather if offers a range of possibilities, a number of suggestions as to what an actor might do. Performances cannot be confined to a single, unalterable realization: rather, each production is continually discovering new potential in a text, and it is this power of revelation and revaluation that the commentary of the Applause Shakespeare seeks to open up to individual readers. With this text in hand, the play can be produced in the theatre of the mind, creating a performance suitable to the moment and responsive to individual imaginations. As stimulus for such recreations, the commentary sometimes describes the choices that particular actors or directors made in famous productions, showing what effect words or physical performances have achieved. The purpose here is to supplement what a reader might supply from his or her own experience and imagination, and also to suggest ways in which further research might discover more about the text's theatrical life.

The commentary is printed in a wide column on the page facing the text itself, so that reference can be quickly made at any particular point or, alternatively, so that the commentary can be read as its own narrative of the play in action. Also, to the right of the text are explanations of difficult words, puns, multiple meanings, topical allusions, references to other texts, etc. All of these things will be found in other editions, but here it is readily accessible without the eye having to seek out the foot of the page or notes bunched together at the rear of the volume. The text is modernized in spelling. Both stage directions and punctuation are kept to a minimum—enough to make reading easy, but not so elaborate that readers are prevented from giving life to the text in whatever way they choose. As an aid to reading aloud, speech-prefixes are printed in full and extra space used to set speeches apart from each other; when the text is read silently, each new voice can register clearly. At the rear of the book, an extended note explains the authority for the text and a collation gives details of variant readings and emendations.

In many ways the Applause Shakespeare is a pioneering edition, responding to an old challenge in a new way and trying to break down barriers to understanding that have proved very obstinate for a long time. Further volumes are in preparation and editorial procedures are being kept under review. Reports on the usefulness of the edition, and especially of its theatrical commentary, would be most welcome. Please write to John Russell Brown, c/o Applause Books, 1841 Broadway, Suite 1100, New York, NY 10023.

INTRODUCTION

The historical events on which *Julius Caesar* is based cover a period of about three years, from October, 45 B.C., to October, 42 B.C. But Shakespeare compressed and transposed what he found in Sir Thomas North's translation of Plutarch's *Lives of the Noble Grecians and Romans* (1579), so that one has the impression that everything takes place in a few days. The play begins with Caesar's triumph, celebrated in October, 45 B.C., for his defeat of Pompey's sons in Spain; this event is combined with the Feast of Lupercal on February 15, 44 B.C. (Act I, scene i). The next sequence (I.ii–III.iii) represents a continuous piece of action, starting with the winning of Brutus to the conspiracy, continuing with the murder of Caesar, and culminating in Antony's funeral oration (with a grotesque aftermath in the death of Cinna the Poet). All of this takes place on the ides of March (March 15, 44 B.C.) and on the day just before it. The complicated happenings of Acts IV and V are telescoped into a few significant scenes that follow one another swiftly. The proscription of the enemies of the Triumvirate (IV.i) occurred in November, 43 B.C., Brutus met Cassius at Sardis early in 42 B.C. and quarreled with him there (IV. ii and iii), and the two battles of Philippi fought in October of the same year are made into a single battle (V.i–v). Shakespeare endows the disparate historical events with a feeling of dramatic and temporal inevitability, and he also convinces us of his fidelity to an authentic vision of ancient Rome.

Julius Caesar can be dated with some assurance in 1599, that critical moment between *Henry V* and *Hamlet* when Shakespeare was at the very mid-point of his career. After the heroic and epic celebration of England in *Henry V*, Shakespeare turned to the best-known crisis of Roman history, and he produced in *Julius Caesar* a play closer to tragedy than any of the English history plays that preceded it. There are obvious differences between English and Roman history, although it is possible that the events surrounding Caesar's assassination were more familiar to the audience than those of the remote English past (the period of *King John*, for example). One of the advantages of looking at *Julius Caesar* from the perspective of the English history plays is that we are likely to find in both many continuities in political, moral, and social assumptions.

This is of special importance on the issue of republicanism. Nothing in Shakespeare's earlier plays suggests that he would find the cause of the conspirators attractive. On the contrary, Brutus and Cassius would seem to be linked with Jack Cade, Northumberland, Worcester, and Scroop as rebels against lawfully constituted authority. Shakespeare was no simple-minded exponent of the Tudor pieties about the divine right of kings, but he did hate the bloodshed and human grief associated with political upheaval. Revolution is associated with a vision of political chaos. The revolutionary cause of Brutus and Cassius has no natural appeal for Shakespeare. To this argument we may add the strongly monarchic sentiments of the English history plays and, in fact, of all Shakespeare's royal plays, even those with weak or evil kings.

Julius Caesar is unique among Shakespeare's works in giving the impression of regicide without actually having a king in it. Its subject is the structure of Roman politics at the near-accession of Caesar, but Shakespeare has adapted his Roman setting to the pattern of ideas in the English history plays, which are in turn a reflection of the realities of Elizabethan England. The presence of the Roman mob in *Julius Caesar* keeps us aware of the public character of the play, since the mob is the final arbiter of political power. The Roman mob is indistinguishable from the English mob of the history plays: they are unwashed, have stinking breaths and greasy caps, are vociferous, violent, capricious, fickle, and, above all, easily moved by any strong appeal to their emotions.

There is an emphasis on public life in *Julius Caesar*, with its appropriate duties, ceremonies, and style of speech, but one always has the sense of a contrast, implied or stated, between the public figure and the private person. Caesar "in his nightgown" (or dressing gown) conversing with his wife Calphurnia or inviting the conspirators—ironically, his "Good friends"—to "go in and taste some wine with me" (II.ii.126) is a very different character from the sardonic demigod of the Senate House putting down Metellus Cimber. And Antony's confidential and personal manner with the mob in his funeral oration proves to be only a calculated public show from which Antony himself stands aloof: "Mischief, thou art afoot,/Take thou what course thou wilt" (III.ii.254–5). This is a chilling anticlimax to the passions of the oration. After the brief but savage interlude of Cinna the Poet (III.iii), we see Antony again with his fellow triumvirs calmly pricking down the names of those who are to die, a bit of horsetrading with the lives of near relatives. Here is politics as naked power, all pretense of human concerns dropped, and the swiftness and lack of sentiment of Act IV, scene i, match the preceding scene of Cinna's absurd murder. Both scenes display the same shocking impersonality and viciousness of the political forces unleashed by Antony's oration.

In Brutus, the public-private conflict begins to develop its potentialities for tragedy. As he admits to Cassius (giving Cassius a wedge to split his resistance), he is "with himself at war" (I.ii.46). This is the generic condition of the tragic protagonist. As he tells Cassius in the quarrel scene, he is "armed so strong in honesty" that all threats, doubts, hesitations, second thoughts, and self-questionings pass by him "as the idle wind" (IV.iii.67–8). This is not literally what he says to Cassius, but one feels sympathetic to Cassius' exasperation with Brutus' four-square, priggish, and overbearing "honesty," the bloody honorableness that Antony exposes so cuttingly in his oration. Brutus' inner conflict ends very abruptly in Act II, scene i, and public determinations replace any private doubts, although there is an air of foredoomed sadness that hangs over Brutus in Acts IV and V. His quarrel with Cassius seems to indicate that the conspiracy has gone sour, its sense of selflessness and dedication swallowed up by talk of money—"so much trash as may be graspèd thus" (IV.iii.26)—and Brutus is beginning to feel his isolation from the other conspirators.

We may say, then, that the tragedy of Brutus lies in the sacrifice of his private self to public and abstract commitments. We cannot argue away the human predicament stated so simply and with such fallible logic in Brutus' soliloquy about Caesar:

> It must be by his death; and for my part,
> I know no personal cause to spurn at him,
> But for the general: he would be crowned. (II.ii.10–12)

"Personal" and "general": this is the basis of Brutus' tragic choice. We know that he will choose the general, public good over any merely personal considerations, in the same generous or overweening spirit in which Caesar tells Artemidorus, "What touches us ourself shall be last served" (III.i.8). Yet I think Shakespeare wants us to grasp that the sacrifice of the personal, human cause to the general, political one always has tragic implications.

Brutus is primarily a sympathetic figure, yet there are many touches to indicate that, unlike the many tragic characters whom he foreshadows (especially Hamlet), he has very limited self-awareness. His garden soliloquy contemplating the death of Caesar is so full of logical flaws that one can only believe that these are intended to characterize Brutus' way of thinking, and Cassius' little plot to win Brutus depends strongly on flattery for its success. Cassius is an anomalous figure in these early scenes, very close to the conventional villain. His soliloquy at the end of Act I, scene ii, has many similarities to those of Iago and Edmund, and we are repelled by his smug gloating over how easy a mark Brutus is.

We are repelled by it because we are convinced that it is true. Brutus is represented as the only innocent idealist among the shrewd and rancorous conspirators; as Antony sums it up in his set speech at the end:

> He only, in a general honest thought
> And common good to all, made one of them. (V.v.71–2)

We are not surprised, therefore, that Brutus should make the three tactical errors that Plutarch notes: he spares Antony's life, he allows Antony to speak a funeral oration for Caesar, and he risks all by engaging the enemy at Philippi. We think the better of Brutus for all these decisions, but we are clearly meant to understand that Cassius would have done otherwise. "That spare Cassius" has the true conspiratorial temperament.

Brutus is sincerely disturbed by the human implications of the conspiracy. "Let's be sacrificers, but not butchers, Caius" (II.i.166), he says, as if he needed to remind Cassius of the true purpose of the conspiracy, as he does later in the quarrel scene (IV.iii). There is much self-indulgence and wish-fulfillment in Brutus' desire to kill Caesar without having "dirty hands." The murder teaches Brutus something about the real nature of killing, and in the exhilaration of the moment he is soon directing his compatriots in an elaborate blood bath:

> Stoop, Romans, stoop,
> And let us bathe our hands in Caesar's blood
> Up to the elbows, and besmear our swords. (III.i.106–8)

"Up to the elbows" seems at first to be hyperbole, but the action indicates that the conspirators are actually "Signed in thy spoil, and crimsoned in thy lethe" (III.i.207), as Antony tells us. He begins his soliloquy by asking Caesar's pardon "That I am meek and gentle with these butchers" (III.i.256). "Butchers" is the direct opposite of "sacrificers," but Brutus himself seems to have abandoned his first notion that the murder could be a clean, priestly sacrifice. If we need further proof of the tragic misdirection of Brutus, we need only listen to the cry of the Third Plebeian after Brutus' oration in the marketplace: "Let him be Caesar" (III.ii.46). This casual identification signifies the utter futility of all that Brutus and the conspirators have done.

As in the case of Richard II, Shakespeare is intent on controlling the audience's feelings toward Caesar, so that his own outrageous *hubris*, or insolence on the largest scale, seems to bring his fate upon him; but once the deed is done, the process is reversed and the insolent king becomes the sacrificial or tragic victim. Caesar's murder is brilliantly set in a context of insufferable pretension, in which he dares publicly to assert his superiority over all other mortal men. "I could be well moved, if I were as you" (III.i.58)—how full of scorn is that condescending gesture, but once Caesar is safely dead he becomes "the ruins of the noblest man/That ever livèd in the tide of times" (III.i.257–8). His physical infirmities, amplified from Plutarch, are forgotten, and in death he is such a potent and hieratic force that he is spoken of as the provider of precious relics.

If history is moral and didactic, as the Elizabethans believed, it could also be a teacher of dark and even paradoxical lessons. We may support the notion that *Julius Caesar* is Shakespeare's most difficult history play by a look at its remarkably ambivalent symbolism. Does the perturbation in nature represented by the storm and its portents serve as a warning of Caesar's tyranny or as an indication of the growing evil of conspiracy in the Roman state? Cassius and Calphurnia read the signs in directly opposite ways, and we are left to draw our own conclusions. Is the bloodletting by the conspirators a way of curing the body politic of its disease of Caesarism, or is it simply the mark of a hideous and brutal murder that must be avenged by more blood? Is the conspiracy a purifying fire that will burn away the "rubbish," "trash," and "offal" of Rome (I.iii.110–11) and make all new, or is it an uncontrollable and diabolic blaze that indiscriminately destroys everything in its path? Our inability to answer these questions with any conviction makes *Julius Caesar* a "problem play."

Although there are many historical errors in *Julius Caesar*, especially anachronisms, Shakespeare did manage to create a convincing sense of ancient Rome. We are made to feel, chiefly through Brutus, that there is a set of characteristically Roman moral qualities: high-mindedness, self-control, the ability to rise above one's material circumstances, fortitude in the face of adversity, moral dedication, constancy of purpose, and a rigorous concern with personal honor. All these are virtues popularly associated with Stoicism in the Renaissance, and even though the Stoics opposed suicide, the willingness to kill oneself rather than live a base life as a captive seems to be a proof of the very resolution and nobility of mind which they admired.

Roman virtue is most admirably and convincingly presented in the domestic scene between Brutus and Portia, as the high-principled daughter of Cato the Utican insists on her prerogatives as Brutus' wife. She has already "made strong proof" of her "constancy," or moral stamina, by giving herself "a voluntary wound/Here, in the thigh" (II.i.299–301)—and the gesture implies a wonderful candor between husband and wife. Brutus, of course, rises to the occasion. His answer to Portia's complaint that she is his "harlot, not his wife" (II.i.287) is in the simple, melodious, and serious style that characterizes this play:

> You are my true and honourable wife,
> As dear to me as are the ruddy drops
> That visit my sad heart. (II.i.288–90)

There are no memorable imaginative flourishes here (or anywhere else in *Julius Caesar*), yet what could be more perfect in tone and feeling for this context? "Ruddy" is a homely word, and the image of Brutus' blood "visiting" his "sad heart"—in Elizabethan English, "sad" is at once sorrowful and grave—carries through the domestic connotations. When Brutus says finally, "0 ye gods!/Render me worthy of this noble wife" (II.i.302–3), we are assured that Portia's "bosom shall partake/The secrets of my heart" (305–6).

The first revelation of Portia's death is placed just at the point where the quarrel between Brutus and Cassius is beginning to wear itself out. Brutus, hinting at darker sorrows than those that have been expressed, says that he is "sick of many griefs" (IV.iii.142), for which Cassius advises him to be philosophical and rise above "accidental evils" (144). Then comes the sudden explosion of Brutus' inner grief: "No man bears sorrow better. Portia is dead" (145). Cassius is stunned—"Ha! Portia?" (146)—and Brutus reiterates with a dirgelike echo: "She is dead" (147). With perfect dramatic tact, Shakespeare has eliminated all empty moralizing from his passage and left the shocking news to carry its own emotional stress, although he does promote the effect of surprise by the prolonged caesura after "better."

These lines seem to vindicate the simple, limited, and tightly controlled Roman style of this play. It is a style that tends to be very literal, without any figures of speech or rhetorical adornments to support its purposes; yet it is often capable of charging the lines with dramatic intensity and conviction. Whatever its imaginative limitations, the Roman style expresses admirably the simple and strong verities of Roman virtue.

Shakespeare's play is based very closely on Sir Thomas North's translation of Plutarch, *The Lives of the Noble Grecians and Romans*, first published in 1579 and reissued in 1595. It seems likely that Shakespeare used the edition of 1595, although the differences between these two editions are minor. Like most Elizabethan translators, North did not go directly to the Greek text of Plutarch, but used the excellent French translation by Jacques Amyot published in 1559. North was no scholar of either Greek or French, but what his version lacks in accuracy it makes up for in vigorous and vivid style. It has the pungency of characterization and liveliness of incidental detail that would make it very attractive to a dramatist looking for material. Shakespeare is sometimes quite close to the phrasing of North; in fact, there are places where he is simply versifying North's prose. Much more significant, however, are Shakespeare's departures from North, where he invents freely or transposes details from a different context.

Shakespeare made direct use of three of Plutarch's "Lives" for his play: Julius Caesar, Marcus Brutus, and Marcus Antonius. "The Life of Marcus

Brutus" was the most important for Shakespeare's purposes, partly because it has so many hints of what was to be Shakespeare's typical tragic protagonist and partly because it is so well written. Shakespeare may also have used details from other "Lives" of Plutarch, such as those of Dion, Cicero, Cato the Younger, and Pompey.

Critics have tended to neglect the comparisons between Grecians and Romans that follow each set of parallel lives. Plutarch's method is to pair a noble Grecian with a noble Roman and then to cap the biographies with a brief comparison of the two in which the superiority of Greek or Roman qualities is debated—and usually decided in favor of the old-fashioned Greek virtues. Thus Brutus is set against Dion, Antony against Demetrius, and, in a comparison that has not survived, Caesar is matched with Alexander the Great. Plutarch shows a wonderful ability in these pairs to make pithy generalizations about character.

It is well to keep in mind that the events surrounding the assassination of Caesar were very well known in Shakespeare's time, so that just about any Elizabethan book may contain some allusion to Caesar or Brutus. North's Plutarch is unquestionably Shakespeare's direct source for *Julius Caesar*, but Shakespeare must have picked up a good deal of information from other sources, including the standard encyclopedias and reference works of the period.

On September 21, 1599, Thomas Platter, a Swiss physician and gentleman traveler, saw a play in London that was almost certainly Shakespeare's *Julius Caesar*. He made this entry in his notebook:

> After lunch on September 21, around two o'clock, I traveled with my party across the water and saw, in the house with the straw-thatched roof, the tragedy of the first emperor, Julius Caesar, skillfully acted by about fifteen persons. At the end of the play, according to their custom, they danced—two in men's costumes and two in women's—most elegantly and admirably with each other.

Since the Globe theater was built in 1599 and opened in the fall, it seems likely that *Julius Caesar* was one of the first plays to be presented there. Besides helping to establish this date, Platter's account gives us some interesting theatrical details: the playhouse was located across the Thames from "the City" of London; "about fifteen persons" could double the thirty-nine or more distinct roles in *Julius Caesar*; and the tragedy was concluded with an elaborate jig.

We can easily understand the play's attractiveness for a foreign visitor and his party. If the number of references to it are a guide to its audience appeal, *Julius Caesar* seems to have been very popular and successful in its own time. It was one of the plays performed at the marriage of Princess Elizabeth and the Elector Palatine in the winter of 1612–13—it is called *Caesars Tragedye* in a court record—and it was played before the King and Queen on January 31, 1637, at St. James, and on November 13, 1638, at the Cockpit.

Julius Caesar maintained its popularity from the Restoration to about the last quarter of the eighteenth century, being produced at least once in almost every year. Its restrained, "classical" style undoubtedly suited the temper of this period; it was never thought necessary to adapt *Julius Caesar* for a more refined age, as so many other plays of Shakespeare were mercilessly altered and rewritten in order to rescue them from their own barbarism. The text of the play, however, was not left without some improvements. One may get a good idea of the *Julius Caesar* most eighteenth-century audiences saw from the acting version printed by John Bell in 1773. To a speech of Brutus taken out of its context and placed at his exit, the editor, Francis Gentleman, has this characteristic note: "Here the transposed lines come in advantageously for the actor's going off." Still, these additions, transpositions, doublings of roles, and deletions are very minor when compared with the drastic adaptation of other Shakespearean plays in the same period.

In the early eighteenth century, *Julius Caesar* was a staple of the repertory of the Theatre Royal in Drury Lane, with Barton Booth notable as Brutus and Robert Wilks as Antony. In the theater in Lincoln's Inn Fields, James Quin was rivaling Booth for his presentation of Brutus, and he played the part many times until 1750. During David Garrick's regime, *Julius Caesar* was never presented at Drury Lane, although he once contemplated acting Cassius. From 1780 to 1812 there are no recorded performances of the play; it seems to have fallen into a decline after a long period of great popularity. It was revived by John Philip Kemble at Covent Garden in 1812 and in each subsequent year to 1817. This production attempted to recreate the splendor of ancient Rome.

Julius Caesar was not a great favorite of the nineteenth-century theater, perhaps for the very reasons that had made it so appealing to neoclassical sensibilities of the Restoration and the eighteenth century. Some memorable renditions of the play were C. M. Young's Brutus, William Charles Macready's Brutus and Cassius, and Samuel Phelps's Brutus and Cassius. Although Macready played Brutus more frequently, he confessed to "a peculiar pleasure" in the role of Cassius "as one among Shakespeare's most perfect specimens of idiosyncrasy." The Royal Theatre of Saxe-Meiningen, on a visit to London, presented *Julius Caesar* at Drury Lane in 1881 with spectacular mob scenes. The review in the *Telegraph* spoke of "those forests of hands and arms, those staccato shouts, that brilliancy of emphasis, the whirl and rout and maddened frenzy of an excited mob."

The most successful nineteenth-century revival of *Julius Caesar* was that of Herbert Beerbohm Tree in 1898 at His Majesty's Theatre, where the play was shown for a hundred nights to enthusiastic audiences. This production was designed and supervised by the painter Sir Lawrence Alma-Tadema, who attempted to picture ancient Rome in all its architectural magnificence. This is not exactly Shakespearean, but one can understand why this splendid production was revived in 1899, in each year from 1905 to 1911, and in 1913. Tree himself played Antony, and he so arranged the play in three acts that he had each of the tableau curtains entirely to himself, thus giving the impression that Antony was the leading part.

For various reasons, perhaps chiefly political, *Julius Caesar* was a more popular play in nineteenth-century America than it was in England. It could have been seen in New York in fifty-one different years in the nineteenth century, and in the period 1835–55 it was revived fifteen times in Philadelphia. Its first production was in Charleston in 1774. Among outstanding actors, Edwin Booth was pre-eminent as Brutus and Laurence Barrett as Cassius; Charles Kean and W. C. Macready also performed in New York. In a memorable performance at the Winter Garden on November 25, 1864, the three Booth brothers acted together in a tercentenary benefit to raise money for a statue of Shakespeare in Central Park. Junius Brutus Booth played Cassius, Edwin Booth played Brutus, and John Wilkes Booth played Antony.

In the twentieth century, *Julius Caesar* has been frequently revived, with most of the leading Shakespearean actors doing a stint as Antony, Brutus, or Cassius. The Mercury Theatre production of Orson Welles, in New York in 1937, put a bold, modern-dress emphasis on the theme of fascism, as did the production at the Embassy Theatre in London in 1939. This inescapable political implication may now seem a barrier to modern directors looking for a fresh interpretation of the play. In 1953 Metro-Goldwyn-Mayer made an impressive movie of *Julius Caesar* directed by Joseph Mankiewicz, with Marlon Brando as Antony, John Gielgud as Cassius, and James Mason as Brutus. Despite the astonishing variety of accents (including Edmond O'Brien's Casca as a Chicago-style gangster) the movie showed insight into the emotional effects of the tragedy.

INTRODUCTION TO COMMENTARY

Shakespeare's *Julius Caesar* is both tragedy and history play, but however readers and critics approach it, stage directors must deal with it as a play written for performance in the theatre.

The Setting

The author of a play to be played in the neutral, architectural theatre of Shakespeare's day had only, in order to set place and time of day, to provide indications early in the dialogue of each scene as to when and where the new unit of action was occurring. Thus, scene design was a matter of words.

Notice how, in the first scene of *Julius Caesar*, Flavius says (l. 3) "...ought not walk/upon a labouring day," and later (l. 27) says, "...lead these men about the streets?" When the time of day changes, at the beginning of Act I, Scene iii, Cicero's first words are, "Good even, Casca." At l. 3 ff., Casca and Cicero both describe the "tempest," setting the scene further, and Cassius, entering later, is greeted by Casca saying, "What night is this!" And so it goes through the plays, with verbal description doing the jobs of defining place and time.

With only an occasional bench or chair to bring on, the action could flow from scene to scene without those stops which the scene changes of the modern theatre so often demand. Also, this neutral stage was utterly flexible, instantly taking on whatever guise the playwright required. At the beginning of Act II, when Brutus enters calling his servant and asking for a taper in his study, we sense right away that we are "at home" with Brutus, and when he talks about the "progress of the stars," we know he is outside and it is still night, as it had been in the previous scene. Shakespeare's audience in the theatre had no need for the written description "in his orchard" which precedes this scene, or for any of the other scenic descriptions which have been placed at the beginnings of scenes to help the reader. The speed and flexibility of Shakespeare's stage allowed him a dramatic structure of swift development and unfettered imagination.

At the Restoration of the monarchy in 1660, Charles II and his courtiers came back from their travels in exile wanting to see plays on the new-fangled Italianate proscenium, or "picture frame," stage. From that time until very recently, proscenium stages were the standard and expected stages for all sorts of dramatic and musical entertainments requiring a theatre. This stage, with its "open mouth," demands scenery to fill it. The art of perspective painting was quick to answer. An interest in archaeology led to "authentic" period settings and costumes for Shakespeare in the 19th Century. Realism and the proscenium theatre abetted one another on into the 20th Century. After World War II, the British director Tyrone Guthrie, having created a production in a Tudor church hall, realized the advantages of the open stage and the three-sided auditorium for Elizabethan drama. At Stratford, Ontario, and later in Minneapolis, he inspired the building of such theatres. Since then, open stages confronting three-sided auditoriums have sprung up across the United States.

For Shakespeare production, that has been a very good thing. The absence of a curtain behind which scenery can be changed forces Shakespeare's speed, flexibility, and scenic neutrality on the modern director and frees him from the constraints of proscenium staging.

This open stage, with the audience on three sides, pushes the director into special choreographic solutions. In the proscenium theatre, actors are arranged in what amounts to a line across the stage so they are all visible from the house simultaneously. With the open stage, if people on the sides are to see, the movement must be circular, like a wheel, instead of back and forth. Too, there must be enough circulation for all the members of the audience to see what is important most of the time. This makes for exciting visual compositions, flowing into each other with ceaselessly vigorous movement. Instead of "tricking" the actors into a straight line, the director can place the important elements center and group the other actors around that center in a much more natural way. Indeed, on such a stage, one can "block" a whole Shakespeare play in one day, by simply telling the actors to stand in a circle and walk toward whomever they are addressing.

Take the assassination scene in *Julius Caesar* (II.i). On the picture frame stage, one would probably place Caesar on a center platform three or four steps tall, with the conspirators and other senators spread out on either side of him. How much more interesting this can look on the open stage, using the same central platform for Caesar, but placing the others in a full circle around him. Each one can speak to Caesar from where he is without regard to "opening up the picture." Casca, who has been deputed to strike first, can get into place behind Caesar without the maneuvering necessary on a picture frame stage, and the confusion after Caesar falls can be arranged much more spectacularly. Then, after Antony enters, he can move to Caesar's body and later to each of the conspirators, ranged in their circle, without the unnatural parading back and forth which the proscenium stage enforces.

Modern directors of Shakespeare must be prepared to mount their productions on both types of stages, or "in-the-round" as well, and very different productions will result, in terms of amount of scenery, nature, and number of properties, and the shape of the stage pictures and movement patterns. While "in-the-round" and the open stage may not be suitable for all types of plays, most modern directors prefer the open stage for Shakespeare.

Historical Period

Julius Caesar is placed in Roman times and is about historical figures from that period. It deals with major events of that time which actually occurred, even though Shakespeare has compressed and interpreted as his artistic needs dictated. It might appear at first glance that no question would then arise as to the period in which the play would be set and costumed.

Since at least the 1920s, however, directors have been transplanting classics, and especially Shakespeare's plays, from their ostensible period to other times, political climates, and modes of behavior.

Today, finding a "resonance" between some other historical time and the play's stated period offers a basis for transplanting period: "as if," say, *The Merchant of Venice* were to take place in a country very like Nazi Germany, with SS men, and concentration camps, and yellow arm bands, and the trappings of "the final solution." Orson Welles, as Maurice Charney notes, set his famed Mercury Theatre production of *Julius Caesar* in a Fascist state, with Brutus and Cassius as reformers bent on overthrowing a dictator. A recent *Julius Caesar* turned Rome into a "banana republic" under the yoke of a Noriega-like strongman.

Such comments on the text can indeed be revealing. Often, however, the attempt to establish relevance to today only obscures the play's special connection with its own time and the way that time can speak to ours.

What seems to me important is that, regardless of directorial or design concepts, the play convey its essential meaning, speak in its own voice clearly, and accomplish for today's audience, insofar as is possible, what its author hoped to do with his.

Visual Elements Essential for *Julius Caesar*

Whatever historical period the director chooses for *Julius Caesar*, or whether he is to work on a proscenium stage, an open stage, or "in-the-round," he must reckon with certain scenic demands the play itself imposes. From its opening through the unleashing of the mob and the following quiet scene with the triumvirs (IV.i), we are in Rome. Suggesting the various places—Brutus' garden, streets, Caesar's house, the Capitol—will probably involve structural elements, realistic or not, which can *contain* the action. Columns, arches, walls, hangings—these can be turned, closed in, opened up, changed in relationship to one another. After IV.i, the play moves out of Rome. The action seems to require open spaces. Brutus' tent (IV.ii) will surely be a portable affair, brought on by soldiers, to be set up at the beginning of the scene and taken away as they leave the tent to go to battle. For the rest of the play, that battlefield is the scene. So, from the end of IV.i, the physical structures which contained Rome must be cleared away, leaving the stage more bare, more open. Solving this need for a transition from containment to openness dictates the physical production for *Julius Caesar*. Not working in the theatre for which Shakespeare's plays were written demands adjustments and compromises which irrevocably individualize each director's production of each of the plays.

What *Julius Caesar* is About

Maurice Charney, in his introduction to the play, has admirably situated *Julius Caesar* among Shakespeare's history plays in terms of a "regicide" upsetting "order" and the play ending with the restoration of that order. He also discusses how Shakespeare gives us an ambiguous picture of Caesar himself in order not to "stack the deck" of the conflict at the outset.

This play is special in that audience interest is divided among three or four chief figures, rather than being focused on a single hero like Hamlet or Macbeth. Brutus, Caesar, Antony, and, though not to quite the same extent, Cassius all occupy the foreground of our interest. This division of interest, I believe, helps to focus audience attention on "process" rather than on "sympathy." Shakespeare apparently wants us to be concerned with "hows" and "whys" rather than with our indentification with "who." This, I think, is why we get a Caesar who is alternately imperious and heroic, monumental and human. Antony is not just a classic "hero" but underneath this surface an astute politician. Cassius is a manipulator, too, with a resemblance to Iago, but he is a passionate admirer of Brutus and patriotically devoted to their cause. Brutus and the rest share noble Roman virtues, but, though Brutus may be "the noblest Roman of them all," Shakespeare gives us here a man attempting to act ethically from an ethically flawed position.

Shakespeare's tragedies and histories usually illuminate through their action some simply-stated moral precept. In the case of *Julius Caesar*, I think the play shows us that "no end is justified which must be attained by evil means." Brutus is the protagonist through whose struggle this thesis is demonstrated. We see him resisting and then being propelled by faulty logic and the influence of others into a course of action which he tries to justify. He falls apart, committing serious practical errors, as he realizes that what he did was wrong. The action of the first part of the play builds through the forming of the conspiracy toward Caesar's murder and its immediate consequence, Antony's swaying of the crowd against the conspirators. The second part of the play deals with the downfall of Brutus and Cassius, which occurs, in part, as a result of Brutus' loss of heart.

Casting

The reader's imaginary enactment of the play will be enhanced by keeping in mind some sense of how its roles might be cast for a production. One need not visualize specific movie greats in particular roles, but being aware of appropriate physical type and emotional tone for the principal parts will help the reader "see" the play as he reads.

Caesar's lean face, thinning hair, his fifty or so years will be familiar to most readers from pictures of busts in history books. The role demands a robust voice and a commanding physical presence, along with enough charisma to mark a leader of men.

Brutus would seem to be in his thirties—athletic, solid, clear-eyed. His speeches would benefit from the round tones of a low baritone voice, secure and masculine.

Cassius, with his "lean and hungry look," is described by Shakespeare. He is the same age as Brutus, and surely tall, with a hawk face. He needs a flexible and resonant voice, probably somewhat more tenor than Brutus', to ensure musical variety in their scenes. There is a mercurial, passionate side of him, too, which the actor must achieve.

Antony must deceive us. "Antony, that revels long a-nights," Caesar calls him. We meet him ready to race in the Lupercal, probably in his late twenties. He is the Antony with whom Cleopatra fell in love. He should look like a glorious, heroic, brainless, Greek statue. He is seen by the others as a mere "play-boy," and only Cassius senses something dangerous beneath the pose. In the young Prince Hal, Shakespeare gives us such a person, but there the audience is shown glimmers along the way of the king who is to come. Antony reveals himself only when he is left alone with the corpse of Caesar, and only after the oration does the audience grasp how astute he really is. Act IV, Scene i shows him as not only clever but ruthless.

Octavius is not introduced until that scene, and we find him young, probably just turned twenty. He is quiet and watchful, and yet his shrewd assessment of Antony at the end of that first scene tells something about the cold and canny young man who will later battle Antony for the known world in *Antony and Cleopatra*.

This is a man's play, and the two women in it are there to shed light on their husbands, who occupy the center of our author's attention. One senses in Portia a woman as much her husband's equal as Shakespeare's time (the time of Queen Elizabeth) would allow. She is meant to embody all those steadfast virtues of the Roman matron literature had made familiar to Elizabethans. Calphurnia, on the other hand, is the younger wife of an older man. Caesar is alternately indulgent and dismissive with her, but he seems to need to appear decisive in her eyes.

Other characters in the play will be cast in relation to their function as conspirators, servants, soldiers, etc., and casting questions of interest will be dealt with in the commentary as they enter.

Does this casting chart seem to suggest a bias toward "type casting"? Certainly it does, if one means that an informed reader would find such choices obvious, because they are the choices suggested by the author's text, his descriptions, and the conflicts in which the characters find themselves. Good casting involves finding actors who can clearly embody the characteristics and tensions in the play, and putting those actors together in a resonant way. No wonderful actor is right for all the wonderful parts. A play is telling a story, and just as it must take place in an appropriate physical environment, so it must be inhabited by people emotionally and physically suitable for the author's characters. Please note that the castings described above are racially color-blind. In today's society and today's theatre, the case has been won for using the best actor available for the part, without regard to *racial* stereotypes. This does not mean that Antony can be successfully played by a 5' 6" wimp, without regard for the physical and emotional attributes Shakespeare wants for his man. The balances and contrasts of the emotional forces within the play must be understood and respected if the casting of the play is to "work."

Other Production Problems

Julius Caesar, like most of the other plays of Shakespeare, offers some problems in production specific to itself. How much blood should there be in which the conspirators bathe their swords? If the actors are in white togas, how do they keep the blood off them? How does one handle the progress from the street into the Capitol just before Caesar's murder? How does one execute the storm so it is effective but also so the actors can be heard? How does one stage Caesar's Ghost? How many actors will constitute a believable mob for the particular production in question?

I have tried to address these and similar questions in context as the reader encounters the problems in the play. My effort throughout has been to help the reader sense *Julius Caesar* as a script for the theatre. The director and actors are involved in an exciting search, a form of detective work, to see what the author intended to happen on stage and how to find modern equivalents to satisfy the play's needs. The commentary which accompanies the text is designed to let the reader in on the pleasures of that search. If the reader finds, as he encounters my notions of how to stage the play and my thoughts about what is going on in the scenes, that he would do the scene or the moment or the staging in some other way, he will have taken his own steps down the path of artistic selection which makes working in the theatre on these great plays so gratifying.

CHARACTERS

JULIUS CAESAR, Roman general
MARCUS ANTONIUS, Caesar's chief supporter
OCTAVIUS CAESAR, a triumvir
M. AEMILIUS LEPIDUS, a triumvir
MARCUS BRUTUS, a leader of the conspiracy
CASSIUS, another leader of the conspiracy

CASCA, TREBONIUS, CAIUS LIGARIUS, DECIUS BRUTUS, METELLUS CIMBER, CINNA, } conspirators

CICERO, POPILIUS LENA, PUBLIUS, } senators

FLAVIUS, MURELLUS, } tribunes

ARTEMIDORUS, teacher of Greek rhetoric

CINNA, poet
MESSALA, friend to Brutus and Cassius
LUCILIUS, one of Brutus' chief officers

VOLUMNIUS, VARRUS, CLAUDIO, CLITUS, STRATO, DARDANIUS, LABIO, FLAVIUS, } officers to Brutus

TITINIUS, one of Cassius' chief officers
PINDARUS, servant to Cassius
YOUNG CATO, son of Marcus Cato
LUCIUS, boy attending on Brutus

CALPHURNIA, wife to Caesar
PORTIA, wife to Brutus

SOOTHSAYER, POET, COBBLER, CARPENTER, OTHER PLEBEIANS, SERVANTS to Caesar, Antony, and Octavius, SENATORS, GUARDS, ATTENDANTS

SCENE *Rome, near Sardis, and near Philippi*

ACT I

Scene i *Enter* Flavius, Murellus, *and certain* Commoners *over the stage.*

Flavius Hence! Home, you idle° creatures, get you home.
Is this a holiday? What, know you not,
Being mechanical,° you ought not walk
Upon a laboring day without the sign
Of your profession?° Speak, what trade art thou?

Carpenter Why, sir, a carpenter.

Murellus Where is thy leather apron and thy rule?°
What dost thou with thy best apparel on?
You, sir, what trade are you?

Cobbler Truly, sir, in respect of° a fine workman, I am but, as you would say, a cobbler.°

Murellus But what trade art thou? Answer me directly.°

Cobbler A trade, sir, that I hope I may use with a safe conscience, which is indeed, sir, a mender of bad soles.°

Murellus What trade, thou knave? Thou naughty° knave, what trade?

Cobbler Nay, I beseech you, sir, be not out° with me; yet if you be out, sir, I can mend you.

Murellus What mean'st thou by that? Mend me, thou saucy fellow?

Cobbler Why, sir, cobble you.

Flavius Thou art a cobbler, art thou?

Cobbler Truly, sir, all that I live by is with the awl. I meddle with no tradesman's matters nor women's matters; but withal° I am indeed, sir, a surgeon to old shoes. When they are in great danger, I recover° them. As proper° men as ever trod upon neat's leather° have gone upon° my handiwork.

Flavius But wherefore art not in thy shop today?
Why dost thou lead these men about the streets?

unoccupied/foolish/trivial

of the working class

occupation, trade

(wordplay on carpenter's rule and self-control)

Stage Directions Although Flavius and Murellus are mentioned first, common sense indicates that they must see those "certain commoners" doing something before they tell them to go home. Although Shakespeare's plays took place on his stage—a stage with no realistic scenery as we know it—it was truly the stage of his imagination. One must always ask of characters in a play, "Why do they come *here?* Why don't they stay out there?" In this instance, *here* is the place where the Lupercalian footrace is to begin, and if, later on, the two tribunes will be "put to silence for pulling scarves off Caesar's images," good stage business would have the carpenter, the cobbler, and their pals putting scarves *on* Caesar's images, which the tribunes can later remove.

in comparison with

(wordplay on mender of shoes and a botcher, bungler)

straightforwardly

(pun on *soles-souls)*

good-for-nothing

(wordplay on out of temper and out at heels)

10-30 The cobbler performs his wordplay, keeping as innocent and straight a face as he can, for the onstage audience of his fellow commoners. This first encounter demonstrates the gulf between the classes in this Rome, with no love lost. The cobbler persists almost to the point of insolence. It is like pulling teeth to get him even to acknowledge his profession outright. Evidently the tribunes are about to lose patience at his last joke (l. 28) about "wearing out their shoes," for he stops kidding and answers directly. This produces not the easy acceptance which his holiday mood might lead him to expect, but an impassioned reprimand.

with awl/ with all/ withal

(pun on shoemaking and medical sense) handsome

cowhide walked

COBBLER Truly, sir, to wear out their shoes, to get myself into more work. But indeed, sir, we make holiday to see Caesar and to rejoice in his triumph.°

MURELLUS Wherefore rejoice? What conquest brings he home?
What tributaries° follow him to Rome
To grace in captive bonds his chariot wheels?
You blocks, you stones, you worse than senseless° things!
O you hard hearts, you cruel men of Rome,
Knew you not Pompey?° Many a time and oft
Have you climbed up to walls and battlements,
To towers and windows, yea, to chimney tops,
Your infants in your arms, and there have sat
The livelong day, with patient expectation,
To see great Pompey pass the streets of Rome.
And when you saw his chariot but appear,
Have you not made an universal shout,
That° Tiber trembled underneath her banks
To hear the replication° of your sounds
Made in her concave shores?
And do you now put on your best attire?
And do you now cull out a holiday?°
And do you now strew flowers in his way
That comes in triumph over Pompey's blood?°
Be gone!
Run to your houses, fall upon your knees,
Pray to the gods to intermit° the plague
That needs must light° on this ingratitude.

FLAVIUS Go, go, good countrymen, and for this fault
Assemble all the poor men of your sort;
Draw them to Tiber banks, and weep your tears
Into the channel, till the lowest stream
Do kiss the most exalted shores° of all.

Exeunt all the Commoners.

See whe'r° their basest mettle° be not moved;
They vanish tongue-tied in their guiltiness.
Go you down that way towards the Capitol;
This way will I. Disrobe the images,°
If you do find them decked with ceremonies.°

Roman victory procession

rich captives who can pay tribute

incapable of feeling/stupid, foolish

Pompey the Great, defeated by Caesar in 48 B.C.

31-54 Murellus' rebuke, chiding the "cruel men of Rome" for their callous forgetting of Pompey, sets the note of patriotism and deep feelings of betrayal which characterize his opposition to Caesar. Immediately we know that these tribunes are not mere villains and traitors, but rather people activated by a cause, and this is the function of the scene—a prologue and background for the coming tempting of Brutus by Cassius. The structure of the speech, the first great verse "aria" of the play, is itself a prologue for the tone of the rugged "Roman" sound which distinguishes the verse of this play from all Shakespeare's other works. Notice the strength of the two questions in lines 31-33, followed by the two and a half lines building to the third question and the name of "Pompey." Next come five and one-half lines as he builds a picture to remind them. The next five lines, from "And when you saw his chariot but appear . . ." ask another question, but note how different it is in tone from the question beginning the speech and the scathing demands which follow in contrast, from line 47, with "And do you now . . ." through to line 51, where he fiercely admonishes them to be gone and expiate the guilt of their ingratitude.

so that

reverberation

i.e., pluck out from working days

the death of Pompey/ Pompey's sons

suspend, delay

alight, fall

55-74 Flavius adds his self-righteous advice to Murellus' fierce commands, and the commoners slink away, probably not so much guilty as wanting to get away before any trouble starts.

highest flood level

whether   substance, nature

60-74 Flavius seems more contemptuous of the mob than Murellus, and also more hotheaded. Flavius (l. 63) suggests disrobing the images. Murellus doubts the wisdom of this, but Flavius sweeps away his objections. His parting words about making Caesar "fly an ordinary pitch" foreshadow Cassius' lines to Brutus about Caesar.

statues

adornments for Caesar's triumph

MURELLUS May we do so?
You know it is the feast of Lupercal.°

FLAVIUS It is no matter; let no images
Be hung with Caesar's trophies.° I'll about°
And drive away the vulgar° from the streets.
So do you too, where you perceive them thick.
These growing feathers plucked from Caesar's wing
Will make him fly an ordinary pitch,°
Who else° would soar above the view of men
And keep us all in servile fearfulness. *Exeunt.*

Scene ii *Enter* CAESAR, ANTONY (*for the course*°), CALPHURNIA, PORTIA, DECIUS, CICERO, BRUTUS, CASSIUS, CASCA, *a* SOOTHSAYER, *[and citizens]. After them,* MURELLUS *and* FLAVIUS.

CAESAR Calphurnia.

CASCA Peace, ho! Caesar speaks.

CAESAR Calphurnia.

CALPHURNIA Here, my lord.

CAESAR Stand you directly in Antonio's way
When he doth run his course. Antonio.

ANTONY Caesar, my lord.

CAESAR Forget not in your speed, Antonio,
To touch Calphurnia; for our elders say,
The barren, touchèd in this holy chase,
Shake off their sterile curse.°

ANTONY I shall remember.
When Caesar says, "Do this," it is performed.

CAESAR Set on, and leave no ceremony out.

SOOTHSAYER Caesar!

CAESAR Ha! Who calls?

CASCA Bid every noise be still. Peace yet again.

Roman fertility festival in February

commemorative ornaments
i.e., I'll go about

commoners

the highest point a falcon soars before it swoops on its prey

otherwise

road race

curse of sterility

Stage Directions Most productions omit the return of Flavius and Murellus, since they do not speak in the coming scene and have clearly gone off on a separate errand at the end of the previous scene, and later in Scene ii Casca speaks of their having been "put to silence." The stage directions imply a procession. Antony is arrayed "for the course." Historical tradition has it that the runners in the race celebrating the Feast of the Lupercal ran naked; for the stage, a loin cloth will do nicely to reveal Antony for the athlete he is. There should probably be other runners, too, all armed with leather thongs with which ceremonially to strike those women who fear barrenness. Why does the procession stop here? Because this is the place the race begins, it would seem. A crowd lines the street, hailing Caesar and awaiting the start of the race. In Roman costume, the white of the senatorial togas, red and gold of the banners, the glint of the soldiers' armor, contrasted with the darker citizens' garments, make this a stirring sight.

1-24 Caesar need not raise his voice; someone is always there to quell the crowd noises. Caesar's opening lines seem to be private, not public, appear to be genial and not severe, and Antony's answer has a gallant ring. After line 11, there is evidently an effort to start the race ("Set on...") and shouting or trumpets or other "ceremony" is implied, for after the Soothsayer's cry, Casca has to ask for "every noise" to be "still." The Soothsayer is either concealed in the crowd or at the far edges of it, for Caesar asks them to "Set him before me," and this implies that the first "Beware the ides of March" is shouted from a distance, in contrast with the more quiet repeat when the man is looking Caesar in the face. Note the foreshadowing as Shakespeare has the still innocent Brutus repeat the Soothsayer's warning before Caesar confronts him. The Soothsayer can be costumed like a wild hermit from the desert, or a *fakir*, and he has been played as a blind "Tiresias." Caesar sees that he is a mystic, either from his dress or his

CAESAR Who is it in the press° that calls on me?
I hear a tongue shriller than all the music
Cry "Caesar!" Speak; Caesar is turned to hear.

SOOTHSAYER Beware the ides° of March.

CAESAR What man is that?

BRUTUS A soothsayer bids you beware the ides of March.

CAESAR Set him before me; let me see his face.

CASSIUS Fellow, come from the throng; look upon Caesar.

CAESAR What say'st thou to me now? Speak once again.

SOOTHSAYER Beware the ides of March.

CAESAR He is a dreamer; let us leave him. Pass.

Sennet.° Exeunt. BRUTUS *and* CASSIUS *remain.*

CASSIUS Will you go see the order° of the course?

BRUTUS Not I.

CASSIUS Pray you do.

BRUTUS I am not gamesome;° I do lack some part
Of that quick° spirit that is in Antony.
Let me not hinder, Cassius, your desires.
I'll leave you.

CASSIUS Brutus, I do observe you now of late.
I have not from your eyes that gentleness
And show of love as I was wont to have.
You bear too stubborn and too strange a hand°
Over your friend that loves you.

BRUTUS Cassius,
Be not deceived. If I have veiled my look,
I turn the trouble of my countenance
Merely° upon myself. Vexèd I am
Of late with passions of some difference,°
Conceptions only proper to myself,
Which give some soil,° perhaps, to my behaviors.
But let not therefore my good friends be grieved
(Among which number, Cassius, be you one),

crowd

mid-point of the month; here March 15

manner. At "Pass," trumpets sound, the ceremonies beginning the race occur, the runners depart, and the procession, with Caesar and Calphurnia in its midst, passes on. This first scene of Caesar's is short, and the author has deliberately kept us from learning much about him. He is clearly head of state, and, in his dealings with the Soothsayer, we sense how he relies on his own instincts, but we have no idea, at this point, whether the author is for or against Caesar. Suspense has been created.

flourish of trumpets

proceedings

fond of sport/frivolous, trivial

lively/swift in running

25-36 Cassius, who with others "in the know" has been keenly alerted by the Soothsayer's warning, is well aware that Brutus has not continued with the procession and "tactfully" invites him to do so. Brutus demurs, with a little wry dig at Antony, the playboy and show-off. He invites Cassius to follow the procession while he himself leaves, but Cassius seizes the occasion to reproach Brutus earnestly for avoiding him. Brutus assures Cassius that he has merely been keeping his troubles to himself but warmly reassures Cassius as to his continued friendship. He seems to be rather pointedly warning Cassius off, though, from any further inquiry. Cassius, however, uses Brutus's reassurance as a springboard for launching his attack on Caesar.

you treat your friend too harshly and too distantly

entirely

strong emotions that conflict with each other

blemish, stain

Nor construe° any further my neglect
Than that poor Brutus, with himself at war,
Forgets the shows° of love to other men.

CASSIUS Then, Brutus, I have much mistook your passion,°
By means whereof this breast of mine hath buried°
Thoughts of great value, worthy° cogitations.
Tell me, good Brutus, can you see your face?

BRUTUS No, Cassius;
For the eye sees not itself but by reflection,
By some other things.

CASSIUS 'Tis just.°
And it is very much lamented, Brutus,
That you have no such mirrors as will turn
Your hidden worthiness into your eye,
That you might see your shadow.° I have heard
Where° many of the best respect° in Rome—
Except immortal Caesar—speaking of Brutus,
And groaning underneath this age's yoke,
Have wished that noble Brutus had his eyes.°

BRUTUS Into what dangers would you lead me, Cassius,
That you would have me seek into myself
For that which is not in me?

CASSIUS Therefore, good Brutus, be prepared to hear.
And since you know you cannot see yourself
So well as by reflection, I, your glass,°
Will modestly discover° to yourself
That of yourself which you yet know not of.
And be not jealous on° me, gentle Brutus.
Were I a common laughter,° or did use
To stale° with ordinary° oaths my love
To every new protester;° if you know
That I do fawn on men and hug them hard,
And after scandal° them; or if you know
That I profess° myself in banqueting
To all the rout,° then hold me dangerous.

Flourish° and shout.

interpret

manifestations

strong feeling, especially sorrow

concealed

weighty

true

reflection, image

i.e., that repute

i.e., was not blind to the real situation in Rome

mirror

will reveal without exaggeration

suspicious of

object of laughter

make cheap or common commonplace/tavern-like

professor

slander

make professions of love

rabble

trumpet fanfare off-stage

48-78 Cassius has often been played as an envious villain, and indeed his soliloquy at the end of this scene reminds one of Iago. It is important to remember that Cassius feels he is in the right. Caesar, in his view, is an aristocrat who has betrayed his class by playing to the mob and creating what a later age would call a "cult of personality." Cassius wants to restore power to the old families and appeals to Brutus as a representative of all that is traditionally noble in the Roman character. His approach to Brutus in this entire section must be reasonable, and, however passionate, earnestly sincere. Actors and directors must never lose sight of the fact that Cassius' energy drives the play, and though the consequences of his conspiracy result in evil, Cassius' intentions were good. He is an intense and manipulative man but not a villain. His first tactic, with Brutus, is to point out in what high respect Brutus is held, and he hints that many would prefer him to Caesar. Brutus is instantly aware that Cassius leads him toward "dangers." Cassius protests the earnest sincerity of his attentions.

BRUTUS What means this shouting?
I do fear the people choose Caesar
For their king.

CASSIUS Ay, do you fear it?
Then must I think you would not have it so.

BRUTUS I would not, Cassius, yet I love him well.
But wherefore do you hold me here so long?
What is it that you would impart to me?
If it be aught toward the general good,°
Set honor in one eye and death i' th' other,
And I will look on both indifferently;°
For let the gods so speed me° as I love
The name of honor more than I fear death.

CASSIUS I know that virtue to be in you, Brutus,
As well as I do know your outward favor.°
Well, honor is the subject of my story.
I cannot tell what you and other men
Think of this life; but for my single self,
I had as lief not be° as live to be
In awe of such a thing as I myself.°
I was born free as Caesar, so were you;
We both have fed as well, and we can both
Endure the winter's cold as well as he.
For once, upon a raw and gusty day,
The troubled Tiber chafing with° her shores,
Caesar said to me, "Dar'st thou, Cassius, now
Leap in with me into this angry flood,
And swim to yonder point?" Upon the word,
Accoutred as I was, I plungèd in
And bade him follow. So indeed he did.
The torrent roared, and we did buffet it
With lusty sinews, throwing it aside
And stemming° it with hearts of controversy.
But ere we could arrive° the point proposed,
Caesar cried, "Help me, Cassius, or I sink."
I, as Aeneas° our great ancestor
Did from the flames of Troy upon his shoulder
The old Anchises° bear, so from the waves of Tiber
Did I the tired Caesar. And this man

79-90 They are interrupted by trumpets and shouting from the direction of the racecourse, and Brutus inadvertently reveals that he fears Caesar will be chosen king. Cassius pounces on this, and with "Then must I think you would not have it so," he directly confronts Brutus with a searching question. Brutus admits his fears, but then he takes the bull by the horns and bluntly demands what Cassius wants of him, charging that it be "for the general good," and consistent with the "name of honor."

public welfare

impartially

make me prosper

appearance, especially of the face

91-132 Cassius begins his denigration of Caesar with a stout assertion that, for himself, he cannot bear to be forced to look up to someone no better than he is. He then tells a story which shows Caesar as a braggart who has to be pulled out of the Tiber as a result of the consequences of his own folly, followed by a slighting reference to Caesar's fever in Spain. The pettiness of these attacks demonstrates the degree of Cassius' envy and of his hurt pride.

would just as soon not be alive

i.e., a mere mortal like myself

raging against

making headway against

arrive at

legendary founder of Rome (hero of Vergil's *Aeneid*)

father of Aeneas

Is now become a god, and Cassius is
A wretched creature, and must bend his body
If Caesar carelessly but nod on him.
He had a fever when he was in Spain,
And when the fit° was on him, I did mark
How he did shake. 'Tis true, this god did shake.
His coward lips did from their color° fly,
And that same eye, whose bend° doth awe the world,
Did lose his° lustre. I did hear him groan.
Ay, and that tongue of his that bade the Romans
Mark him, and write his speeches in their books,
"Alas !" it cried, "Give me some drink, Titinius,"
As a sick girl. Ye gods, it doth amaze° me
A man of such a feeble temper° should
So get the start of° the majestic world,
And bear the palm° alone. *Shout. Flourish.*

BRUTUS Another general shout?
I do believe that these applauses are
For some new honors that are heaped on Caesar.

CASSIUS Why, man, he doth bestride the narrow world
Like a Colossus,° and we petty men
Walk under his huge legs, and peep about
To find ourselves dishonorable graves.
Men at some time are masters of their fates.
The fault, dear Brutus, is not in our stars,
But in ourselves, that we are underlings.
"Brutus" and "Caesar." What should be in that "Caesar"?
Why should that name be sounded° more than yours?
Write them together: yours is as fair a name.
Sound them: it doth become the mouth as well.
Weigh them: it is as heavy. Conjure with 'em:
"Brutus" will start° a spirit as soon as "Caesar."
Now in the names of all the gods at once,
Upon what meat° doth this our Caesar feed
That he is grown so great? Age, thou art shamed.
Rome, thou hast lost the breed of noble bloods.°
When went there by an age, since the great flood,°
But it was famed with more than with one man?
When could they say, till now, that talked of Rome,

ague

natural color (red)/flag

glance

its

bewilder, stupefy

temperament

outstrip

Roman emblem of victory

133-178 Another shout and flourish of trumpets interrupts him, confirming Brutus' fear that the public is giving Caesar some new honor. Cassius proceeds to compare Brutus and Caesar as equally worthy, and passionately denounces the present age for putting up with the domination of a mere man who takes upon himself the prerogatives of kingship. Brutus quietly hears him out. When Cassius finally comes to a fiery conclusion, Brutus thanks him for his regard, assures him he will consider what has been said and will, in time, give his answer. He cannot help, it would seem, adding that he too is not about to put up with what seems to lie ahead. Throughout this scene between Cassius and Brutus—two men earnestly talking, in contrast to the bustle and ceremony which has gone before—there is a contrast between the impassioned, vivid speech of the mercurial Cassius and the steady, reasoned utterance of Brutus. This makes the touches of feeling which break through Brutus' calm—his expressions of concern at the shouts and his "Brutus had rather be a villager" comment—all the more telling. Cassius, it seems, brings the conversation to a close, well satisfied with the result.

bronze statue of Apollo, more than 100 feet high, which spanned the harbor of Rhodes

pronounced/resounded/proclaimed

rouse

a general Elizabethan word for food

persons of spirit

Zeus destroyed all of mankind by flood except Deucalion and Pyrrha

That her wide walks encompassed but one man?
Now is it Rome indeed, and room° enough,
When there is in it but one only man.
O, you and I have heard our fathers say
There was a Brutus° once that would have brooked°
Th' eternal devil to keep his state° in Rome
As easily as a king.

BRUTUS That you do love me, I am nothing jealous;°
What you would work me to, I have some aim;°
How I have thought of this, and of these times,
I shall recount hereafter. For this present,
I would not so°—with love I might entreat you—
Be any further moved.° What you have said,
I will consider; what you have to say,
I will with patience hear, and find a time
Both meet° to hear and answer such high things.
Till then, my noble friend, chew upon° this:
Brutus had rather be a villager
Than to repute himself a son of Rome
Under these hard conditions as° this time
Is like to lay upon us.

CASSIUS I am glad that my weak words
Have struck but thus much show of fire° from Brutus.

Enter CAESAR *and his train.*°

BRUTUS The games are done, and Caesar is returning.

CASSIUS As they pass by, pluck Casca by the sleeve°
And he will, after his sour fashion, tell you
What hath proceeded worthy note today.

BRUTUS I will do so. But look you, Cassius,
The angry spot doth glow on Caesar's brow,
And all the rest look like a chidden° train.
Calphurnia's cheek is pale, and Cicero
Looks with such ferret° and such fiery eyes
As we have seen him in the Capitol,
Being crossed in conference° by some senators.

CASSIUS Casca will tell us what the matter is.

(pun on *Rome-room*, which were pronounced alike)

Lucius Junius Brutus, who drove the Tarquins from Rome endured

royal court

suspicious, doubtful

guess, conjecture

thus

urged

fitting

ruminate, ponder

which

(Brutus is imagined as the flint)

retinue

(togas had no sleeves; Shakespeare is thinking of the Elizabethan doublet)

rebuked

a small animal with red eyes used to hunt rabbits

debate

179-190 At line 179, it seems Cassius stops because he is aware of the returning procession. Brutus' line is probably not a warning that Cassius should stop talking, but a comment on the early and surprising return of the ceremonial procession. Cassius and Brutus speak aside as the stage fills with Caesar and his attendants. From the presence of these asides (which surely couldn't be spoken over the earlier flourishes and shouts) as well as from Brutus' reference to the "chidden train," it appears that this crowd entrance is a silent one, in contrast to the joyous ceremonies of the earlier appearance of Caesar. Brutus and Cassius will have moved to the side to watch the approach of the "royal" party, and from there they speak their asides, plucking Casca by the sleeve as he passes them.

CAESAR Antonio.

ANTONY Caesar.

CAESAR Let me have men about me that are fat,
Sleek-headed° men, and such as sleep a-nights.
Yond Cassius has a lean and hungry look;
He thinks too much. Such men are dangerous.

ANTONY Fear him not, Caesar, he's not dangerous.
He is a noble Roman, and well given.°

CAESAR Would he were fatter! But I fear him not.
Yet if my name were liable to fear,
I do not know the man I should avoid
So soon as that spare Cassius. He reads much,
He is a great observer, and he looks
Quite through the deeds of men.° He loves no plays,
As thou dost, Antony; he hears no music.
Seldom he smiles, and smiles in such a sort
As if he mocked himself, and scorned his spirit
That could be moved to smile at anything.
Such men as he be never at heart's ease°
Whiles they behold a greater than themselves,
And therefore are they very dangerous.
I rather tell thee what is to be feared
Than what I fear; for always I am Caesar.
Come on my right hand, for this ear is deaf,°
And tell me truly what thou think'st of him.

Sennet. Exeunt CAESAR *and his train.*

CASCA You pulled me by the cloak; would you speak with me?

BRUTUS Ay, Casca, tell us what hath chanced today
That Caesar looks so sad.°

CASCA Why, you were with him, were you not?

BRUTUS I should not then ask Casca what had chanced.

CASCA Why, there was a crown offered him; and being offered him, he put it by with the back of his hand, thus; and then the people fell a-shouting.

BRUTUS What was the second noise for?

191-211 Caesar, from the center, calls brusquely for Antony, who responds promptly. It appears that Brutus and Cassius, who have just spoken "aside," unheard by Caesar, are not meant to hear Caesar's discussion with Antony, and if they can't then no one else can. In other words, the entire procession waits in silence while Caesar confers confidentially with Antony. Cassius cannot avoid noticing that he is being referred to, so there is tension in the air. When Caesar speaks of Cassius being "dangerous," Antony confidently reassures Caesar: "Fear him not." Caesar quickly says, "I fear him not," and then asserts, "Yet if my name were liable to fear . . ." Here is a hint of that imperial manner which Cassius so resents, but the whole exchange is dark with what seems to be Caesar's ill humor about the way things went while the procession was at the racecourse. It may be, too, that the Soothsayer's warning is still ringing in Caesar's ears, and the sight of Cassius standing aside has awakened concerns Caesar wants to share.

smooth-haired

disposed

i.e., Cassius has good psychological insight into men's motives

212-215 Caesar shakes off his appearance of concern with another assertion of superiority—"for always I am Caesar"—and then immediately follows with the reference to "this ear is deaf," which may be Shakespeare's way of reminding the audience that Caesar is mortal after all. Unconsciously, his Caesar moves from the almost-godlike to an acknowledgement of human weakness. Shakespeare could also intend this auditory symptom to be understood as a temporary consequence of the epileptic fit which Casca soon tells about , but the effect is, in any case, a touch of genius. A striking thing about the play, thus far, is how little the author has shown us about Caesar. Are we to see him as hero or villain? So far Shakespeare has been deliberately equivocal, because the play is not going to be about Caesar, but about the effect his assassination will have on those around him. Since Orson Welles' Mercury Theatre production in the 1930's, some modern directors have followed in Welles' footsteps and portrayed Caesar as a demagogic fascist dictator and Brutus and Cassius as liberal patriots. This appears to "stack the cards" in a way Shakespeare was trying to avoid. If the history of it matters at all, it is as well to remember that Caesar was the one breaking down class barriers, and that Brutus and Cassius were leaders of a reactionary revolution.

contented, tranquil

(not mentioned in any ancient authority)

serious

216-227 Casca, of whom Brutus will say, "What a blunt fellow this is grown to be," has been played as a disdainful effeminate fop, perhaps because he

CASCA Why, for that too.

CASSIUS They shouted thrice. What was the last cry for?

CASCA Why, for that too.

BRUTUS Was the crown offered him thrice?

CASCA Ay, marry,° was't, and he put it by thrice, every time gentler than other; and at every putting-by mine honest° neighbors shouted.

CASSIUS Who offered him the crown?

CASCA Why, Antony.

BRUTUS Tell us the manner of it, gentle Casca.

CASCA I can as well be hanged as tell the manner of it: it was mere foolery; I did not mark it. I saw Mark Antony offer him a crown—yet 'twas not a crown neither, 'twas one of these coronets°—and, as I told you, he put it by once; but for all that, to my thinking, he would fain° have had it. Then he offered it to him again; then he put it by again; but to my thinking, he was very loath to lay his fingers off it. And then he offered it the third time. He put it the third time by; and still° as he refused it, the rabblement° hooted,° and clapped their chopt° hands, and threw up their sweaty nightcaps, and uttered such a deal of stinking breath because Caesar refused the crown, that it had, almost, choked Caesar; for he swounded° and fell down at it. And for mine own part, I durst not laugh, for fear of opening my lips and receiving the bad air.

CASSIUS But soft,° I pray you. What, did Caesar swound?

CASCA He fell down in the market place and foamed at mouth and was speechless.

BRUTUS 'Tis very like° he hath the falling sickness.°

CASSIUS No, Caesar hath it not; but you, and I,
And honest Casca, we have the falling sickness.

CASCA I know not what you mean by that, but I am sure Caesar fell down. If the tag-rag people° did not clap him and hiss him, according as he pleased and displeased them, as they use to do the players in the theatre, I am no true° man.

speaks harshly of the rabblement and their "stinking breath" and "sweaty nightcaps." The scene is effective enough in the theatre when he is played that way, but it should be noted that the only prose passage prior to Casca's speeches are the lines of the cobbler and carpenter in the first scene. The other prose passages are the Brutus oration, where a sense of direct and unvarnished honesty is achieved, and the murder of Cinna the Poet, where the effect is one of brutality. For the rest, the play is in verse. It seems, therefore, that Casca's prose is meant to emphasize his bluntness, his "calling a spade a spade," and to support his rough-hewn choice of words. Between line 215 and line 227, Casca simply describes what happened, without much personal detail, as if trying to remain objective and neutral.

228-288 At line 228, Brutus seems surprised and displeased—and Casca, at "every time gentler than other," for the first time seems to color his story. Cassius, who knows more about Casca's sympathies than Brutus does, asks who pressed the crown on Caesar. Brutus, whose sympathies are unknown to Casca, wants more details. Casca, at first cautious ("I can as well be hanged as tell the manner of it"), warms to his theme, perhaps emboldened by the presence of Cassius, whose sympathies he does know. As Casca fills out his description of the crown offering, he becomes increasingly ironic. He ironically affects not to understand Cassius' reference to everybody having the falling sickness, but then describes Caesar's performance in increasingly contemptuous terms. He passes off Cassius' question about Cicero with a joke, but is direct and serious with the news about Flavius and Murellus being "put to silence." He deals with Cassius' dinner invitation with his customary affectation of crudeness, and leaves.

indeed (a mild oath, "By the Virgin Mary")

honorable, worthy

little crowns (Shakespeare seems to be thinking of Tudor coronets)

gladly

ever, every time   rabble

shouted (their approval)

chapped

swooned

just a moment (a vague Elizabethan interjection)

likely   epilepsy

ragged riffraff

honest

BRUTUS What said he when he came unto himself?

CASCA Marry, before he fell down, when he perceived the common herd was glad he refused the crown, he plucked me° ope his doublet° and offered them his throat to cut. And° I had been a man of any occupation, if I would not have taken him at a word, I would I might go to hell among the rogues. And so he fell. When he came to himself again, he said, if he had done or said anything amiss, he desired their worships to think it was his infirmity.° Three or four wenches where I stood cried, "Alas, good soul!" and forgave him with all their hearts. But there's no heed to be taken of them; if Caesar had stabbed their mothers, they would have done no less.

BRUTUS And after that, he came thus sad away?

CASCA Ay.

CASSIUS Did Cicero say anything?

CASCA Ay, he spoke Greek.

CASSIUS To what effect?

CASCA Nay, and I tell you that, I'll ne'er look you i' th' face again. But those that understood him smiled at one another and shook their heads; but for mine own part, it was Greek to me.° I could tell you more news too. Murellus and Flavius, for pulling scarfs off Caesar's images, are put to silence.° Fare you well. There was more foolery yet, if I could remember it.

CASSIUS Will you sup with me tonight, Casca?

CASCA No, I am promised forth.

CASSIUS Will you dine with me tomorrow?

CASCA Ay, if I be alive, and your mind hold,° and your dinner worth the eating.

CASSIUS Good; I will expect you.

CASCA Do so. Farewell both. *Exit.*

BRUTUS What a blunt° fellow is this grown to be!
He was quick mettle° when he went to school.

i.e., plucked

a short, close-fitting Elizabethan jacket   if

i.e., the falling sickness

(proverbial in Shakespeare's time for something incomprehensible)

suppressed

does not change

slow-witted

of a lively disposition

289-301 Brutus tests Cassius about Casca, and Cassius elliptically confirms that Casca's heart is in the right place, in spite of his "front." Brutus accepts this and prepares to leave, making it quite clear that

CASSIUS So is he now, in execution
Of any bold or noble enterprise,
However he puts on the tardy form.°
This rudeness° is a sauce to his good wit,
Which gives men stomach° to disgest° his words
With better appetite.

BRUTUS And so it is. For this time I will leave you.
Tomorrow, if you please to speak with me,
I will come home to you; or if you will,
Come home to me, and I will wait for you.

CASSIUS I will do so. Till then, think of the world.°

Exit BRUTUS.

Well, Brutus, thou art noble; yet I see
Thy honorable mettle° may be wrought
From that it is disposed. Therefore it is meet°
That noble minds keep ever with their likes;
For who so firm that cannot be seduced?
Caesar doth bear me hard,° but he loves Brutus.
If I were Brutus now and he were Cassius,
He° should not humor me.° I will this night,
In several hands,° in at his windows throw,
As if they came from several citizens,
Writings, all tending to the great opinion
That Rome holds of his name; wherein obscurely
Caesar's ambition shall be glancèd at.
And after this, let Caesar seat him sure,
For we shall shake him, or worse days° endure. Exit.

Scene iii *Thunder and lightning. Enter* CASCA *and* CICERO *[at different doors].*

CICERO Good even, Casca. Brought you Caesar home?
Why are you breathless, and why stare you so?

he is willing to meet with Cassius to carry on what has begun. Cassius agrees, urging Brutus significantly to think about all that is at stake. Brutus leaves without a reply. Cassius no doubt looks after him for a moment.

guise of slowness and stupidity

roughness

appetite digest

i.e., the present state of the world

302-316 The actor playing Cassius will probably want to look after Brutus as he says the first lines of his soliloquy, but, at "therefore it is meet...", in an Elizabethan staging, he would turn to speak directly to the audience. A soliloquy spoken thus becomes either a discussion in which the speaker works out his thesis answering the unspoken thoughts of his audience or an expository speech in which he gives them information. This Cassius speech combines both functions. Here is one way it could work: Beginning with: "Therefore it is meet..." he could remind the audience of something they, and Brutus, ought to be wary of. Then, at "Caesar doth bear me hard," he could weigh a truth he knows. At "If I were Brutus now..." he could wryly comment on Brutus' naivete. Next, at "I will this night..." he reveals a decision. The last lines, at "And after this..." could be a burning promise of things to come. A soliloquy can also be done as a stream of consciousness, a "talking to oneself," but these speeches seem to gain in theatricality when given in direct address.

disposition, temperament

fitting

has a grudge against me

i.e., Brutus win me over

handwritings

i.e., even worse than Caesar's present tyranny

Stage Directions Shakespeare rarely begins a new scene with a character on the stage who ended the preceding scene. The plot-advancing portion of this scene begins when Cassius enters, but the exigencies of playing in full light on an open stage led Shakespeare to start this scene with someone else (Cicero) meeting Casca. Through his presence, Casca establishes the storm and the supernatural events which Cassius will later use. Modern stage technology has enabled us to create realistic thunder and lightning for these scenes, but they create their

CASCA Are not you moved, when all the sway° of earth
Shakes like a thing unfirm? O Cicero,
I have seen tempests, when the scolding winds
Have rived° the knotty oaks, and I have seen
Th' ambitious ocean swell and rage and foam,
To be exalted with° the threat'ning clouds;
But never till tonight, never till now,
Did I go through a tempest dropping fire.
Either there is a civil strife in heaven,
Or else the world, too saucy° with the gods,
Incenses them to send destruction.

CICERO Why, saw you anything more wonderful?

CASCA A common slave—you know him well by sight—
Held up his left hand, which did flame and burn
Like twenty torches joined; and yet his hand,
Not sensible of° fire, remained unscorched.
Besides—I ha' not since put up° my sword—
Against° the Capitol I met a lion,
Who gazed° upon me, and went surly by
Without annoying° me. And there were drawn
Upon a heap° a hundred ghastly° women,
Transformèd with their fear, who swore they saw
Men, all in fire, walk up and down the streets.
And yesterday the bird of night° did sit,
Even at noonday, upon the market place,
Hooting and shrieking. When these prodigies°
Do so conjointly meet,° let not men say,
"These are their reasons, they are natural,"
For I believe they are portentous things
Unto the climate° that they point upon.

CICERO Indeed, it is a strange-disposèd° time.
But men may construe things after their fashion,
Clean from the purpose° of the things themselves.
Comes Caesar to the Capitol tomorrow?

CASCA He doth; for he did bid Antonio
Send word to you he would be there tomorrow.

CICERO Good night then, Casca.
This disturbèd sky is not to walk in.

realm, dominion

split

elevated to

insolent

sensitive to

sheathed

opposite

gazed fixedly, stared

harming

huddled together looking like ghosts

screech owl

unnatural, portentous events

coincide

region

abnormal

opposite to the meaning

own problems. If one realistically depicts such a storm, how can one make the actors audible? Shakespeare's stage conventions allowed his audience to believe in a storm created by poetic imagery.

1-41 Shakespeare wanted the supernatural elements introduced in this scene and referred to as portents by Calphurnia in her later scene with Caesar in order to raise the question of the involvement of "the gods" and "the stars" and Fate in the affairs of men, although his Cicero seems not as superstitious as Casca. Wanting to emphasize the humanly tragic aspects of the play, I have, in all five of my productions of it, cut the Cicero portion, beginning the scene with thunder, Casca entering to take shelter under a portico, followed by Cassius entering from the other side, unsure of who is already there. We do lose Cicero establishing Caesar's visit next day to the Capitol, but that is sufficiently established later. Shakespeare production is a process involving artistic decisions and therefore a matter of compromises. "Win a little, lose a little"—with taste as the arbiter.

CASCA Farewell, Cicero. *Exit* CICERO.

Enter CASSIUS.

CASSIUS Who's there?

CASCA A Roman.

CASSIUS Casca, by your voice.

CASCA Your ear is good. Cassius, what night° is this!

CASSIUS A very pleasing night to honest men.

CASCA Who ever knew the heavens menace so?

CASSIUS Those that have known the earth so full of faults.
For my part, I have walked about the streets,
Submitting me unto the perilous night,
And thus unbracèd,° Casca, as you see,
Have bared my bosom to the thunder-stone;°
And when the cross° blue lightning seemed to open
The breast of heaven, I did present myself
Even in the aim° and very flash of it.

CASCA But wherefore did you so much tempt the heavens?
It is the part° of men to fear and tremble
When the most mighty gods by tokens send
Such dreadful heralds to astonish° us.

CASSIUS You are dull, Casca,
And those sparks of life that should be in a Roman
You do want, or else you use not.
You look pale, and gaze, and put on° fear,
And cast yourself in wonder,
To see the strange impatience of the heavens;
But if you would consider the true cause—
Why all these fires; why all these gliding ghosts;
Why birds and beasts, from quality and kind;°
Why old men, fools, and children calculate;°
Why all these things change from their ordinance,°
Their natures, and preformèd faculties,°
To monstrous° quality—why, you shall find
That heaven hath infused them with these spirits°

42-73 Casca and Cassius, on the deserted streets in the dark of night, and both aware of the dangers in the political as well as in the natural environment, are wary until they have identified each other. Casca is fearful, shaken by the night's sights and sounds. In contrast, Cassius is exhilarated. (I have always cut l.64 through l.73, wanting to make this scene as short as possible because of the thunder and lightning problems, and also in order to reduce the supernatural emphasis. Remember that for the modern theatre and modern audiences, Shakespeare's plays are long, and unless we are doing them in a festival or academic situation where uncut fidelity is part of audience expectation, then our necessary cuts must serve our interpretation as well as support audience attention.)

i.e., what a night

with doublet unbuttoned

thunderbolt

forked, zigzag

i.e., at the point at which the lightning seemed to be aimed

function, role

stun, dismay

show, display

contrary to their characteristic nature

prophesy by studying astrological signs

preordained order

inherent qualities or powers

unnatural

powers

To make them instruments of fear and warning
Unto some monstrous state.
Now could I, Casca, name to thee a man
Most like this dreadful night,
That thunders, lightens, opens graves, and roars
As doth the lion in the Capitol;
A man no mightier than thyself or me
In personal action, yet prodigious° grown,
And fearful,° as these strange eruptions° are.

CASCA 'Tis Caesar that you mean, is it not, Cassius?

CASSIUS Let it be who it is; for Romans now
Have thews° and limbs like to their ancestors.
But woe the while!° Our fathers' minds are dead,
And we are governed with our mothers' spirits;
Our yoke and sufferance° show us womanish.

CASCA Indeed, they say the senators tomorrow
Mean to establish Caesar as a king;
And he shall wear his crown by sea and land
In every place, save here in Italy.

CASSIUS I know where I will wear this dagger then;
Cassius from bondage will deliver Cassius.
Therein,° ye gods, you make the weak most strong;
Therein, ye gods, you tyrants do defeat.
Nor stony tower, nor walls of beaten brass,
Nor airless dungeon, nor strong links of iron,
Can be retentive° to the strength of spirit;
But life, being weary of these worldly bars,
Never lacks power to dismiss itself.
If I know this, know all the world° besides,
That part of tyranny that I do bear
I can shake off at pleasure. *Thunder still.*°

CASCA So can I.
So every bondman° in his own hand bears
The power to cancel° his captivity.

CASSIUS And why should Caesar be a tyrant then?
Poor man, I know he would not be a wolf
But that he sees the Romans are but sheep;

74-132 From line 74, "Now, could I, Casca, name to thee a man..." Cassius seems to challenge Casca to declare himself on the side of the conspirators. Casca is still cautious—" 'Tis Caesar that you mean...?" and also in his probing speech about the senate meaning to establish Caesar as a king. Cassius declares himself further, passionately vowing suicide rather than submission. Casca replies, still equivocally, that even a slave can do as much. After one more fervent outburst, having so far failed to elicit any declaration from Casca, Cassius vows to defend himself against Casca should Casca prove, after all, to be a "willing bondman." Only at this point does Casca stoutly declare himself to be with the conspirators. Shakespeare's holding this declaration in suspense has helped hold the audience through the earlier material about politics and the state of nature. Now, very quickly, Cassius lets Casca know a meeting is afoot, and hard upon this comes Cinna's entrance, building the pace and tension. Notice, though, how Shakespeare, just before Cinna's entrance, brings the scene full circle with Cassius' last reference to "this fearful night."

like a prodigy, portentous

causing fear violent outbursts

sinews

alas for these times

i.e., our meek and patient endurance of our subjugation

i.e., in suicide

hold in, confine

i.e., let all the world know

constantly

slave

annul (with wordplay on *bond* as a legal agreement)

He were no lion, were not Romans hinds.°
Those that with haste will make a mighty fire
Begin it with weak straws. What trash° is Rome,
What rubbish and what offal,° when it serves
For the base matter to illuminate
So vile° a thing as Caesar! But, O grief,
Where hast thou led me? I, perhaps, speak this
Before a willing bondman;° then I know
My answer must be made. But I am armed,
And dangers are to me indifferent.°

CASCA You speak to Casca, and to such a man
That is no fleering° telltale. Hold, my hand.
Be factious° for redress of all these griefs°
And I will set this foot of mine as far
As who goes farthest.

CASSIUS There's a bargain made.
Now know you, Casca, I have moved° already
Some certain of the noblest minded Romans
To undergo° with me an enterprise
Of honorable-dangerous consequence;
And I do know by this, they stay for me
In Pompey's porch;° for now, this fearful night,
There is no stir or walking in the streets,
And the complexion of the element°
In favor's° like the work we have in hand,
Most bloody, fiery, and most terrible.

Enter CINNA.

CASCA Stand close° awhile, for here comes one in haste.

CASSIUS 'Tis Cinna; I do know him by his gait.
He is a friend. Cinna, where haste you so?

CINNA To find out you. Who's that, Metellus Cimber?

CASSIUS No, it is Casca, one incorporate
To° our attempts. Am I not stayed for,° Cinna?

CINNA I am glad on't.° What a fearful night is this
There's two or three of us have seen strange sights.

female deer/base menials/ rustics

wood used for kindling

refuse, garbage

worthless

i.e., if Casca is a "willing bondman," he will also be an informer on Cassius

of no concern

sneering, mocking

form a faction or political party grievances

persuaded

undertake

i.e., the portico of the theater built by Pompey in 55 B.C.

appearance of the sky

in appearance is

out of sight

133-153 Now, with Cinna's entrance, the atmosphere of conspiracy and danger is heightened. "Stand close," and "Who's that, Metellus Cimber?" along with Cinna's nervousness about the night and the repetition of Cassius' "Am I not stayed for?" heighten the tension further, framing the urgency of winning Brutus and the importance of Cassius' precise instructions about the papers he has prepared.

intimately bound up with waited for

of it

CASSIUS Am I not stayed for? Tell me.

CINNA Yes, you are. O Cassius,
If you could but win the noble Brutus
To our party—

CASSIUS Be you content. Good Cinna, take this paper,
And look you lay it in the praetor's chair,°
Where Brutus may but find it;° and throw this
In at his window; set this up with wax
Upon old Brutus'° statue. All this done,
Repair to Pompey's porch, where you shall find us.
Is Decius Brutus° and Trebonius there?

CINNA All but Metellus Cimber, and he's gone
To seek you at your house. Well, I will hie,°
And so bestow these papers as you bade me.

CASSIUS That done, repair to Pompey's theatre. *Exit* CINNA.
Come, Casca, you and I will yet, ere day,
See Brutus at his house. Three parts of him
Is ours already, and the man entire
Upon the next encounter yields him ours.°

CASCA O, he sits high in all the people's hearts;
And that which would appear offence in us,
His countenance,° like richest alchemy,
Will change to virtue and to worthiness.

CASSIUS Him and his worth and our great need of him
You have right well conceited.° Let us go,
For it is after midnight, and ere day
We will awake him and be sure of him. *Exeunt.*

official seat of the highest-ranking judicial magistrate

i.e., only Brutus may find it

Brutus' ancestor, Lucius Junius Brutus

Decimus Brutus (Shakespeare takes over the error from North's Plutarch)

hasten

154-166 Cinna leaves, and at line 155 Cassius shares with the newly enlisted Casca the plan to see Brutus at his house. Casca reinforces how important Brutus can be to the cause, and as they leave, Cassius gives us the time, ". . . after midnight," so that the pressure of their intended visit to Brutus ("ere day") hangs over the beginning of the next scene.

surrenders

approval

very well judged

ACT II

Scene i *Enter* Brutus *in his orchard.*°

Brutus What, Lucius, ho!
I cannot, by the progress of the stars,
Give guess how near to day. Lucius, I say!
I would it were my fault to sleep so soundly.
When, Lucius, when? Awake, I say! What, Lucius!

Enter Lucius.

Lucius Called you, my lord?

Brutus Get me a taper° in my study, Lucius;
When it is lighted, come and call me here.

Lucius I will, my lord. *Exit.*

Brutus It must be by his death; and for my part,
I know no personal cause to spurn at° him,
But for the general:° he would be crowned.
How that might change his nature, there's the question.
It is the bright day that brings forth the adder,
And that craves° wary walking. Crown him—that—
And then I grant we put a sting in him,
That at his will he may do danger° with.
Th' abuse of greatness is, when it disjoins
Remorse° from power. And to speak truth of Caesar,
I have not known when his affections swayed°
More than his reason. But 'tis a common proof°
That lowliness° is young ambition's ladder,
Whereto the climber upward turns his face;
But when he once attains the upmost round,°
He then unto the ladder turns his back,
Looks in the clouds, scorning the base degrees°
By which he did ascend. So Caesar may;
Then lest he may, prevent.° And since the quarrel
Will bear no color for the thing he is,°
Fashion it thus: that what he is, augmented,
Would run to these and these extremities;°

garden

candle

Stage directions "Enter Brutus in his orchard." The Elizabethan stage offered few opportunities for physical changes in the setting, and certainly nothing new is needed to play the coming scene, not even an added chair. With Cassius' exit reinforcing the time, and Brutus entering with a reference to a darkness so deep that he cannot see the stars, the poet has given us all the scenery we need, and then by calling to Lucius, a nearby servant, and asking for candle to be placed in his study, Brutus suggests to us that we are indeed outside but in a private garden or courtyard.

be scornful to

public (as opposed to "personal")

requires

harm

pity, compassion

passions ruled

truth drawn from ordinary experience

humility

rung

lower rungs

anticipate and thereby forestall

i.e., since the case against Caesar cannot be justified in relation to Caesar as he is now

extremes

10-35 Once again, the play gives us a soliloquy which develops an argument. Understood in the first line is the premise that "there is no other way to accomplish unseating Caesar except by assassinating him." The rest of the speech is a series of "pro's" and "con's" by means of which Brutus leads himself to justify his thesis. Here again is a speech which can be played as a stream of consciousness, a "talking aloud to oneself." The directness of the Elizabethan stage, however, gave this speech the form of a dialogue with the audience, whose thoughts and questions are silent. This must have enforced on the audience an awareness of Brutus making his tragically wrong choice of trying to achieve a good end by evil means. This choice sets in motion the events which follow—events resulting in the failure of Brutus' cause and his own destruction. With the speech given in direct address, the audience would be on the edge of saying, "No, don't do it," instead of passively listening to a stream of consciousness. At lines 14-15, is one of those small actor choices on which much thought and critical ink have been spent. Is one to suppose that "the bright day brings forth the adder and also (or therefore) requires one to walk carefully," or that "the bright day is the kind of day that brings forth the adder, and *that* kind of day requires that we walk carefully"? Perhaps the answer here can be found, as so often with these questions, by scanning the line. Have we an anapest: "and that

And therefore think him as a serpent's egg,
Which hatched, would as his kind° grow mischievous,
And kill him in the shell.

Enter LUCIUS.

LUCIUS The taper burneth in your closet,° sir.
Searching the window for a flint, I found
This paper, thus sealed up, and I am sure
It did not lie there when I went to bed.

Gives him the letter.

BRUTUS Get you to bed again, it is not day.
Is not tomorrow, boy, the ides of March?

LUCIUS I know not, sir.

BRUTUS Look in the calendar and bring me word.

LUCIUS I will, sir. *Exit.*

BRUTUS The exhalations,° whizzing in the air,
Give so much light that I may read by them.

Opens the letter and reads.

"Brutus, thou sleep'st. Awake, and see thyself.
Shall Rome, &c.° Speak, strike, redress!
Brutus, thou sleep'st. Awake!"
Such instigations have been often dropped
Where I have took them up.
"Shall Rome, &c." Thus must I piece it out:°
Shall Rome stand under one man's awe?° What, Rome?
My ancestors did from the streets of Rome
The Tarquin drive, when he was called a king.
"Speak, strike, redress!" Am I entreated
To speak and strike? O Rome, I make thee promise,
If the redress will follow, thou receivest
Thy full petition° at the hand of Brutus.

Enter LUCIUS.

LUCIUS Sir, March is wasted fifteen days. *Knock within.*°

craves" or an iamb: "and *that/* craves *wa/*ry *walk/*ing? And then note the scansion of the rest of the line and what happens to the repeated "that" which changes its meaning: "*Crown/* him—*that—/*" (crown him king —imagine *that* untenable state of affairs!) Examining such details is the actor's path toward finding the author's intended reading. The speech concludes with the "adder" image—the serpent's egg—by means of which Brutus vanquishes his own best feelings—"And to speak truth of Caesar, / I have not known when his affections swayed / More than his reason," and "...since the quarrel / Will bear no color for the thing he is"—and finds justification in these speculations, overriding his misgivings.

because of its nature

private room, study

35-43 Lucius returns, bearing with him one of the papers we have just seen Cassius give to Cinna. As Brutus dismisses Lucius, he makes a connection between what he has been thinking, the unopened "paper," and the Soothsayer's recent warning, hence his question about "the ides of March."

meteors

44-45 Having just made sure the audience knows how dark the night is, Shakespeare must use the earlier-planted celestial phenomena to let Brutus read his anonymous letter.

spoken in full: *et cetera*

fill in the blank represented by "&c"

i.e., be in awe of one man

46-58 Cassius' device of the anonymous letter, plus the others "dropped" where he has "took them up," pushes Brutus over the edge, from abstract justification to a vow of action. The appeal is to Brutus's pride of family and sense of public duty. The trick works, and, at the end of this speech, with "Am I entreated to speak and strike?" and "If the redress will follow. thou receivest / Thy full petition..." Brutus *accepts* the premise that the end justifies the means.

all you ask

off-stage

59-60 On the heels of this decision, Lucius confirms the "fatal" coincidence of the conspiracy with the Soothsayer's warning, and just as promptly comes the sharp and significant knocking at the outer gate which signals, as the audience knows, the arrival of the conspirators. Lucius goes. All this is highly theatrical and effective in terms of heightening the tension.

BRUTUS 'Tis good. Go to the gate; somebody knocks.

[Exit LUCIUS.*]*

Since Cassius first did whet° me against Caesar,
I have not slept.
Between the acting of a dreadful thing
And the first motion,° all the interim is
Like a phantasma° or a hideous dream.
The Genius° and the mortal instruments°
Are then in council;° and the state of a man,
Like to a little kingdom,° suffers then
The nature of° an insurrection.

Enter LUCIUS.

LUCIUS Sir, 'tis your brother° Cassius at the door,
Who doth desire to see you.

BRUTUS Is he alone?

LUCIUS No, sir, there are moe° with him.

BRUTUS Do you know them?

LUCIUS No, sir; their hats are plucked about their ears
And half their faces buried in their cloaks,
That by no means I may discover° them
By any mark of favor.°

BRUTUS Let 'em enter. *[Exit* LUCIUS.*]*
They are the faction.° O conspiracy,
Sham'st thou to show thy dang'rous brow by night,
When evils are most free?° O then, by day
Where wilt thou find a cavern dark enough
To mask thy monstrous visage? Seek none, conspiracy;
Hide it in smiles and affability.
For if thou path,° thy native semblance on,°
Not Erebus° itself were dim enough
To hide thee from prevention.°

incite

prompting, impulse

nightmare, illusion

guardian spirit of a man

man's faculties

deliberating

i.e., a microcosm of that larger kingdom of the body politic

a kind of

61-69 This parenthetical speech of Brutus while waiting for the decisive meeting with the conspirators also heightens tension—Brutus is poised on the brink, balanced between decision and action. He describes his own state as like a kingdom in the midst of an unresolved revolution. In spite of his private decision, he could still go back.

brother-in-law (Cassius was married to Junia, the sister of Brutus)

more

70-85 Lucius, entering, brings news of Cassius requesting a late-night audience. Brutus guesses that he may not be alone, and Lucius confirms, apparently troubled by the mysterious masked visitors. Brutus firmly accepts their visit. Again, while waiting, Brutus shares with the audience his misgivings about the means he will have to use, the dissembling to which they must, as conspirators, resort. Thus the playwright again tightens the screws of suspense.

recognize

appearance, especially of the face

political party

evil things can range about most freely

walk

showing yourself as you really are

the classical hell (between Earth and Hades)

being discovered

Enter the conspirators, CASSIUS, CASCA, DECIUS, CINNA, METELLUS, *and* TREBONIUS.

CASSIUS I think we are too bold upon° your rest.
Good morrow, Brutus, do we trouble you?

BRUTUS I have been up this hour, awake all night.
Know I these men that come along with you?

CASSIUS Yes, every man of them; and no man here
But honors you; and every one doth wish
You had but that opinion of yourself
Which every noble Roman bears of you.
This is Trebonius.

BRUTUS He is welcome hither.

CASSIUS This, Decius Brutus.

BRUTUS He is welcome too.

CASSIUS This, Casca; this, Cinna; and this, Metellus Cimber.

BRUTUS They are all welcome.
What watchful° cares do interpose themselves
Betwixt your eyes and night?

CASSIUS Shall I entreat a word?

They whisper.

DECIUS Here lies the east. Doth not the day break here?

CASCA No.

CINNA O pardon, sir, it doth; and yon grey lines
That fret° the clouds are messengers of day.

CASCA You shall confess that you are both deceived.
Here, as I point my sword, the sun arises,
Which is a great way growing on° the south,
Weighing° the youthful season of the year.
Some two months hence, up higher toward the north
He first presents his fire; and the high° east
Stands as the Capitol, directly here.

BRUTUS Give me your hands all over, one by one.

86-100 The clump of muffled conspirators enters. Only Cassius is revealed fully, the rest having their (Elizabethan) hats pulled down and their cloaks rucked up about their faces, as Lucius has described. We have a pretty good idea, from a rough sketch of a *Titus Andronicus* performance made by an audience member, that a mixture of Roman and contemporaneous clothing was worn on the Elizabethan stage, but usually in Shakespeare's plays, when reference is made to costume, it is Elizabethan garments which are described. If a production were to be done in Roman garb, dark cloaks could be worn in this scene over the senatorial white togas, with hoods on the cloaks pulled up to cover the heads and shadow the faces. Cassius' tone indicates the seriousness of his visit. Brutus demands the identity of his visitors, and Cassius earnestly assures Brutus of their devotion to Brutus. He solemnly introduces them, one by one, and the implication is that each reveals his face as he is introduced. It is also effective if each comes down to Brutus as he does so, looking Brutus squarely in the eye. This moment of confrontation will be echoed later when Antony takes the bloody hands of the same men, confronting them after the assassination.

i.e., in intruding upon

The audience is meant to assume, it would appear, that each of these men commands important influence and position in the Senate. Their involvement with the conspiracy gives it credence. Brutus asks, "What do you want?" in that formal and convoluted fashion which Shakespeare often uses when characters are concealing their thoughts or know more than they are saying. Cassius takes him aside.

that keep you awake

100-111 These curious lines cover the conversation of Brutus and Cassius, not heard by the audience. Perhaps they are meant simply to fill in necessary waiting time. The author could have devised some useful lines about the conspiracy. Why didn't he? He has gone to great effort to keep the suspense going up to now. Note that Decius begins the interlude—Decius, the one they later select because of his tact to be sure Caesar really goes to the Capitol. Perhaps here he intervenes tactfully to give the others something to talk about so they won't seem to be overhearing the important invitation Cassius is extending to Brutus. Casca, with his characteristic bluntness, sets them straight, while possibly Decius is more closely watching Brutus and Cassius than paying attention to Casca.

interlace, adorn

encroaching on

considering

due

112-140 Brutus, in asking for their hands, signals his joining their conspiracy. Cassius, with what is

CASSIUS And let us swear our resolution.

BRUTUS No, not an oath. If not the face of men,°
The sufferance° of our souls, the time's abuse—°
If these be motives weak, break off betimes,°
And every man hence to his idle bed.°
So let high-sighted° tyranny range° on
Till each man drop by lottery.° But if these,°
As I am sure they do, bear fire enough
To kindle cowards, and to steel with valor
The melting° spirits of women, then, countrymen,
What need we any spur but our own cause
To prick° us to redress? What other bond
Than secret Romans° that have spoke the word°
And will not palter?° And what other oath
Than honesty° to honesty engaged°
That this shall be or we will fall for it?
Swear° priests and cowards and men cautelous,°
Old feeble carrions° and such suffering° souls
That welcome wrongs. Unto bad causes swear
Such creatures as men doubt; but do not stain
The even° virtue of our enterprise,
Nor th' insuppressive mettle° of our spirits,
To think that or our cause or° our performance
Did need an oath; when every drop of blood
That every Roman bears, and nobly bears,
Is guilty of a several bastardy°
If he do break the smallest particle
Of any promise that hath passed from him.

CASSIUS But what of Cicero? Shall we sound him?
I think he will stand very strong with us.

CASCA Let us not leave him out.

CINNA No, by no means.

METELLUS O let us have him, for his silver hairs°
Will purchase us a good opinion,°
And buy men's voices to commend our deeds.
It shall be said his judgement ruled our hands.
Our youths and wildness shall no whit° appear,
But all be buried in his gravity.°

i.e., the look of oppression on the faces of Roman citizens
suffering the corruption of these times
at once
i.e., bed of idleness
arrogant, haughty fly in search of prey
chance i.e., these motives

yielding, passive

incite
i.e., Romans capable of secrecy pledged ourselves
equivocate
personal honor pledged
i.e., let such unworthy persons swear crafty
old men with one foot in the grave patient in endurance
uniform
unsuppressible courage
either... or

i.e., each drop of Roman blood will prove that it is of bastard, non-Roman origin

i.e., both his age and his unblemished reputation
reputation

not in the least
authoritative sobriety

surely a normal impulse for strengthening the ties binding them, proposes an oath, and here Brutus, for the first of several times, asserts his authority by contradicting Cassius. He is saying, "If we don't care enough about our country's wrongs to right them, let's go home. But if these men are as committed as I know they are, we don't need an oath." Having said it clearly by line 128, he says it again, in different words, suggesting to many modern directors that a cut someplace here would not be amiss. Still, why does Shakespeare have him go on so long about these rather abstract questions of honor?

141-153 There may be a clue to the answer in this sequence about Cicero. Cassius makes a practical suggestion that Cicero, whom we met earlier, be included, on the basis of his influence, his standing, and judgement. Note the brevity with which Brutus deals with this practical matter, abrupt and brusque. And what about the reason Brutus gives? Who is it who seems unwilling to follow anything that other men begin but Brutus himself? In spite of the aspects of nobility Shakespeare wants us to see in Brutus, he seems also to be revealing some flaws in his character. Cassius immediately accedes to Brutus, however, and the others quickly follow his lead.

BRUTUS O name him not; let us not break with° him,
For he will never follow anything
That other men begin.

CASSIUS Then leave him out.

CASCA Indeed, he is not fit.

DECIUS Shall no man else be touched, but only Caesar?

CASSIUS Decius, well urged.° I think it is not meet
Mark Antony, so well beloved of Caesar,
Should outlive Caesar; we shall find of him°
A shrewd contriver.° And you know, his means,°
If he improve° them, may well stretch so far
As to annoy° us all; which to prevent,°
Let Antony and Caesar fall together.

BRUTUS Our course will seem too bloody, Caius Cassius,
To cut the head off and then hack the limbs—°
Like wrath in death and envy° afterwards;
For Antony is but a limb of Caesar.
Let's be sacrificers, but not butchers, Caius.
We all stand up against the spirit of Caesar,°
And in the spirit of men there is no blood.
O that we then could come by° Caesar's spirit
And not dismember Caesar! But, alas,
Caesar must bleed for it. And, gentle° friends,
Let's kill him boldly, but not wrathfully;
Let's carve him as a dish fit for the gods,
Not hew him as a carcass fit for hounds.
And let our hearts, as subtle masters do,
Stir up their servants to an act of rage,
And after seem to chide 'em. This shall make
Our purpose necessary, and not envious;°
Which so appearing to the common eyes,
We shall be called purgers,° not murderers.
And for Mark Antony, think not of him;
For he can do no more than Caesar's arm
When Caesar's head is off.

CASSIUS Yet I fear him,
For in the ingrafted° love he bears to Caesar—

disclose our purposes to

suggested

in him

dangerous plotter resources (especially military)

make good use of

harm anticipate and thereby forestall

dependent branches or bodily members

malice

Caesarism/Caesar's soul (in contrast to his body)

get possession of

having the qualities of a gentleman

malicious

bloodletters

deeply implanted

154-191 Now Decius raises the matter of Antony, and, on cue, Cassius urges that Antony be killed along with Caesar. Brutus immediately vetoes this most practical suggestion on the grounds of principle. This is most peculiar, for having accepted, in principle, that the concept of assassination is justified in this instance, Brutus now balks at ensuring its success by all necessary means. After trying to inspire his co-conspirators with the virtues of "killing with deep regret," he supports his position with a misreading of Antony which will prove to be fatal to their cause. This time Cassius protests vigorously, and Brutus does not even let him finish his sentence. Rather than lose Brutus through a confrontation over this or any issue, the conspirators accept his view.

BRUTUS Alas, good Cassius, do not think of him.
If he love Caesar, all that he can do
Is to himself: take thought° and die for Caesar;
And that were much he should,° for he is given
To sports, to wildness, and much company.

TREBONIUS There is no fear° in him; let him not die,
For he will live, and laugh at this hereafter.

Clock strikes.°

BRUTUS Peace! Count the clock.

CASSIUS The clock hath stricken three.

TREBONIUS 'Tis time to part.

CASSIUS But it is doubtful yet
Whether Caesar will come forth today or no;
For he is superstitious grown of late,
Quite from the main° opinion he held once
Of fantasy,° of dreams, and ceremonies.°
It may be these apparent°prodigies,
The unaccustomed terror of this night,
And the persuasion of his augurers°
May hold him from the Capitol today.

DECIUS Never fear that. If he be so resolved,
I can o'ersway him;° for he loves to hear
That unicorns may be betrayed with trees,°
And bears with glasses,° elephants with holes,°
Lions with toils,° and men with flatterers.
But when I tell him he hates flatterers,
He says he does, being then most flatterèd.
Let me work;
For I can give humor° the true bent,°
And I will bring him to the Capitol.

CASSIUS Nay, we will all of us be there to fetch him.

BRUTUS By the eighth hour; is that the uttermost?°

CINNA Be that the uttermost, and fail not then.

METELLUS Caius Ligarius doth bear Caesar hard,°

become melancholy

i.e., too much for him

i.e., nothing to be feared

(an obviously Elizabethan detail)

192-193 The clock strikes, and Brutus, assuming leadership, alerts them to it. The implication is that their business is over, and Trebonius obediently sets their departure in motion. Cassius is apt to get an unwanted laugh on "The clock hath stricken three," if the clock is audible, as it must be, to audience as well as actors. Nothing is lost if the line is cut.

193-222 Cassius raises the genuinely urgent question as to Caesar's attendance at the Capitol, because of the possible influence of the apparently supernatural events of the preceding night on Caesar's newly superstitious nature. Decius takes on the task of ensuring that he comes, reminding them of Caesar's accessibility to suggestion and flattery. Brutus stays out of this discussion, but, when it is over, he sets the time of meeting Caesar.

very different from the strong

fancy portents, omens

manifest

augurs, priests who studied omens

overrule him by persuasion

(according to tradition, the unicorn could be tricked into impaling its horn in a tree)

mirrors pitfalls

nets, snares

disposition, inclination proper turn

latest

215-220 Metellus suggests involving Caius Ligarius, and Brutus receives this suggestion with enthusiasm, almost as if his warmth here could make up for his earlier negativism.

has a grudge against Caesar

Who rated° him for speaking well of Pompey.
I wonder none of you have thought of him.

BRUTUS Now, good Metellus, go along by him.°
He loves me well, and I have given him reasons;
Send him but hither, and I'll fashion° him.

CASSIUS The morning comes upon's. We'll leave you, Brutus.
And, friends, disperse yourselves; but all remember
What you have said, and show yourselves true Romans.

BRUTUS Good gentlemen, look fresh and merrily.
Let not our looks put on° our purposes,
But bear it° as our Roman actors do,
With untired spirits and formal constancy.°
And so good morrow to you every one.

Exeunt. BRUTUS *remains.*

Boy! Lucius! Fast asleep? It is no matter;
Enjoy the honey-heavy dew of slumber.°
Thou hast no figures nor no fantasies°
Which busy care draws in the brains of men;
Therefore thou sleep'st so sound.

Enter PORTIA.

PORTIA Brutus, my lord.

BRUTUS Portia! What mean you? Wherefore rise you now?
It is not for your health thus to commit°
Your weak condition° to the raw cold morning.

PORTIA Nor for yours neither. Y'have ungently°, Brutus,
Stole from my bed. And yesternight at supper
You suddenly arose and walked about,
Musing and sighing, with your arms across;°
And when I asked you what the matter was,
You stared upon me with ungentle looks.
I urged you further; then you scratched your head,
And too impatiently stamped with your foot.
Yet I insisted, yet you answered not,
But with an angry wafter° of your hand
Gave sign for me to leave you. So I did,

berated

i.e., by his house

shape (to the conspiracy)

show, display

i. e., play your parts

dignified self-possession

224-228 As the conspirators muffle themselves in their cloaks preparing to depart, Brutus, as leader, reminds them not to give themselves away—instead, to be like good Roman actors. They leave.

i.e., a sweet, deep, and refreshing sleep

dream images which "busy care" produces

229-233 Brutus either sees Lucius where he has fallen asleep out of view of the audience, or assumes, because Lucius doesn't come when he's called, that he must be asleep. In any case, Lucius must not be distractingly visible asleep on stage during either the conspirator's scene or Portia's scene coming up.

233-236 Portia enters. Brutus is surprised to see her awake, and, urging her "weak condition," wants her to go indoors.

expose

constitution

in a manner not befitting a gentleman

i.e., folded across your chest (a sign of melancholy)

waving

237-302 Instead of going, she presents the evidence of her own eyes that, from "yesternight at supper," he has been behaving strangely. Shakespeare was quite willing to use a device more than once if it served him, and for another scene in which another wife whose husband is involved in a conspiracy marshalls evidence of his own behavior against him, the reader may refer to Lady Percy confronting Hotspur in *Henry IV*, *Part One*, Act II, Scene iii. Hotspur, too, tries to evade wifely pressure, but where that scene turns comedic, this one becomes more serious. Brutus says he is sick. Portia refutes that on the basis of his remaining in the unhealthy night air, and then demands, on the basis of their marriage vows, that

Fearing to strengthen that impatience
Which seemed too much enkindled; and withal°
Hoping it was but an effect of humor,°
Which sometime hath his° hour with every man.
It will not let you eat, nor talk, nor sleep;
And could it work so much upon your shape°
As it hath much prevailed on your condition,°
I should not know you Brutus.° Dear my lord,
Make me acquainted with your cause of grief.

BRUTUS I am not well in health, and that is all.

PORTIA Brutus is wise and, were he not in health,
He would embrace° the means to come by it.

BRUTUS Why, so I do. Good Portia, go to bed.

PORTIA Is Brutus sick? And is it physical°
To walk unbraced° and suck up the humors°
Of the dank morning? What, is Brutus sick?
And will he steal out of his wholesome bed
To dare the vile contagion of the night,°
And tempt° the rheumy and unpurgèd° air
To add unto his sickness? No, my Brutus,
You have some sick offence° within your mind,
Which by the right and virtue° of my place
I ought to know of; and upon my knees,
I charm° you, by my once commended beauty,
By all your vows of love, and that great vow
Which did incorporate° and make us one,
That you unfold° to me, your self, your half,
Why you are heavy°—and what men tonight
Have had resort to you; for here have been
Some six or seven, who did hide their faces
Even from darkness.

BRUTUS Kneel not, gentle Portia.

PORTIA I should not need, if you were gentle Brutus.
Within the bond of marriage, tell me, Brutus,
Is it excepted° I should know no secrets
That appertain to you? Am I your self
But, as it were, in sort or limitation?°

by right he must confide in her. She then confronts him with her knowledge that men, masking their faces, have been to see him. He still resists. She accuses him of treating her like a harlot, not a wife. He protests that he honors her as his wife. She asserts her special strength, as wife to Brutus and daughter to Cato. Finally she cites the "voluntary wound" in her thigh. According to Plutarch, the source of this tale, she deliberately cut herself with a razor, as a result of which she came down with a fever, which could be the "weak condition" to which Brutus referred. Recovering, she used her self-inflicted wound as evidence to Brutus that she had the fortitude to keep his secret. In the play, it does seem to be the mention of the wound which moves Brutus to promise to share his troubles with her, however unclear it may be as to whether he knew of it as the scene begins. For the stage the problem becomes quite practical. Does Portia merely gesture politely toward her thigh? Does she reveal her thigh wrapped with a bloody bandage? Has she just inflicted the cut and does it, unbandaged, bleed freshly? Does she show Brutus an upstage leg the audience cannot see? On the stage, the boldest choice is often the best choice, but this whole wound business is quite unpleasant for modern audiences. Since Brutus seems to change because she presents her wound, the reference cannot be cut without damaging Shakespeare's structure.

besides

product of whim

its

physical appearance

disposition

i.e., know you to be Brutus

take, adopt

healthful

with doublet unbuttoned

dampness, mist

capacity of the night air to infect

risk

damp and unpurified

harmful sickness

power, prerogative

entreat earnestly, conjure

make one body of us

disclose

sad, dejected

made an exception

conditionally or with restricted tenure (legal)

To keep° with you at meals, comfort your bed,
And talk to you sometimes? Dwell I but in the suburbs°
Of your good pleasure? If it be no more,
Portia is Brutus' harlot, not his wife.

BRUTUS You are my true and honorable wife,
As dear to me as are the ruddy drops
That visit my sad heart.

PORTIA If this were true, then should I know this secret.
I grant I am a woman; but withal°
A woman that Lord Brutus took to wife.
I grant I am a woman; but withal
A woman well reputed, Cato's daughter.°
Think you I am no stronger than my sex,
Being so fathered and so husbanded?
Tell me your counsels,° I will not disclose 'em.
I have made strong proof° of my constancy,°
Giving myself a voluntary wound
Here, in the thigh. Can I bear that with patience,
And not my husband's secrets?

BRUTUS O ye gods
Render me worthy of this noble wife. *Knock.*
Hark, hark, one knocks. Portia, go in awhile,
And by and by thy bosom shall partake
The secrets of my heart.
All my engagements° I will construe° to thee,
All the charactery of my sad brows.°
Leave me with haste. *Exit* PORTIA.
Lucius, who's that knocks?

Enter LUCIUS *and* LIGARIUS.

LUCIUS Here is a sick man that would speak with you.

BRUTUS Caius Ligarius, that Metellus spake of.
Boy, stand aside. Caius Ligarius, how?°

LIGARIUS Vouchsafe° good morrow from a feeble tongue.

BRUTUS O what a time have you chose out brave° Caius,
To wear a kerchief!° Would you were not sick!

i.e., keep company

outskirts

at the same time

(Marcus Porcius Cato, Brutus' uncle as well as father-in-law, known for the strict integrity of his life)

secrets

test, trial fortitude

303-309 What is particularly interesting here is that the significant knocking (second time for this play, and don't forget the knocking in *Macbeth*) interrupts the opportunity for Brutus to tell all, and in spite of the promise he makes to "construe" all his engagements, he shortly leaves with Ligarius without telling poor Portia a thing.

commitments explain in detail

what is written in characters on the grave furrows of my forehead

310-334 Lucius, awakened out by the gate by the knocking, brings Caius Ligarius. The theatrically effective device of the sick man made well brings the end of this scene off with vigor if it is executed without apology. The "kerchief," or bandage around the forehead, was a conventional stage symbol for sickness. If Ligarius wears one and even carries a stick and speaks in feeble tones, he can cast aside stick and kerchief at "I here discard my sickness," and speak heartily. Of course it will get a laugh, but a

how are you?

deign to accept

i.e., noble

to be sick

LIGARIUS I am not sick, if Brutus have in hand
Any exploit worthy the name of honor.

BRUTUS Such an exploit have I in hand, Ligarius,
Had you a healthful ear to hear of it.

LIGARIUS By all the gods that Romans bow before,
I here discard my sickness. Soul of Rome,
Brave son, derived from honorable loins,°
Thou like an exorcist hast conjured up
My mortifièd° spirit. Now bid me run,
And I will strive with things impossible,
Yea, get the better of them. What's to do?

BRUTUS A piece of work that will make sick men whole°

LIGARIUS But are not some whole that we must make sick?°

BRUTUS That must we also. What it is, my Caius,
I shall unfold° to thee, as we are going
To whom° it must be done.

LIGARIUS Set on° your foot,
And with a heart new-fired I follow you,
To do I know not what; but it sufficeth
That Brutus leads me on. *Thunder.*

BRUTUS Follow me then. *Exeunt.*

Scene ii *Thunder and lightning. Enter* JULIUS CAESAR *in his nightgown.*°

CAESAR Nor heaven nor earth have been at peace tonight.
Thrice hath Calphurnia in her sleep cried out,
"Help, ho! They murder Caesar!" Who's within?

Enter a SERVANT.

SERVANT My lord.

CAESAR Go bid the priests do present° sacrifice,
And bring me their opinions of success.°

sympathetic one. "But are not some whole that we must make sick," will also get a chuckle. He and Brutus, rising to the occasion, can get into the exit lines with zest and energy, and the end of the scene points forward with mounting intensity toward the assassination we know is coming.

i.e., descended from Lucius Junius Brutus

deadened

healthy

i.e., kill (a euphemism)

disclose

i.e., to the house of the person to whom

advance

Stage Directions Thunder and Lightning are called for. Thunder was possible in Shakespeare's theatre, probably created by rolling a cannon ball down a wooden trough, but the lightning was of course beyond them. Notice that the "thunder" picks up the end of the previous scene and "bridges" into this one, as sound is used as a bridging device today. In this instance, it serves to tell the audience that the time from one scene to the other is continuous.

dressing gown

1-6 Caesar's first line supports the sense of one continuous and troubled night. His concern with Calphurnia's sleeping cry and his asking for the priests to advise about the nature of the day ahead support the suspense the author is at pains to sustain.

immediate

results

SERVANT I will, my lord. *Exit.*

Enter CALPHURNIA.

CALPHURNIA What mean you, Caesar? Think you to walk forth?
You shall not stir out of your house today.

CAESAR Caesar shall forth; the things that threatened me
Ne'er looked but on my back. When they shall see
The face of Caesar, they are vanishèd.

CALPHURNIA Caesar, I never stood on ceremonies,°
Yet now they fright me. There is one within,
Besides the things that we have heard and seen,
Recounts most horrid sights seen by the watch.°
A lioness hath whelpèd in the streets,
And graves have yawned and yielded up their dead.
Fierce fiery warriors fight upon the clouds
In ranks and squadrons and right form of war,°
Which drizzled blood upon the Capitol.
The noise of battle hurtled° in the air,
Horses did neigh, and dying men did groan,
And ghosts did shriek and squeal° about the streets.
O Caesar, these things are beyond all use,°
And I do fear them.

CAESAR What can be avoided
Whose end is purposed by the mighty gods?
Yet Caesar shall go forth; for these predictions
Are to° the world in general as to Caesar.

CALPHURNIA When beggars die, there are no comets seen;
The heavens themselves blaze forth° the death of princes.

CAESAR Cowards die many times before their deaths;
The valiant never taste of death but once.
Of all the wonders that I yet have heard,
It seems to me most strange that men should fear,
Seeing that death, a necessary end,
Will come when it will come.

Enter a SERVANT.

What say the augurers?

attached importance to omens or portents

night watchmen

true and proper military order

clashed

(according to classical tradition, ghosts had thin, shrill, piercing voices)

that which is usual, normal

i.e., are applicable to

proclaim/make a fiery display of

8-37 Calphurnia must enter in time to hear Caesar's instructions to the servant. She puts her foot down, insisting that Caesar stay home. Caesar's immediate response is to contradict her, asserting his will and his courage. Now, anyone producing the play will have to decide how old Calphurnia is, in order to cast the part. Her age has clearly an important effect on how the scene is played and on the relationship between her and Caesar. Shakespeare gives us no help, except to imply, in Act I, Sc. ii, that she is of childbearing age. History tells us that Caesar had two previous wives, but North's translation of Plutarch, Shakespeare's Roman source, gives us little information about Calphurnia. Going beyond the history available to Shakespeare tells us little about his *plays*, and such research often interferes with our reading *the play itself* with proper attention. Shakespeare's history plays are not history—but plays, with their own internal integrity. So—here we have two wives, contrasted. Portia reasons with her husband and then asserts her rights and claims what is due her based on the richness of the marriage. Calphurnia shares her superstitious fears and pleads with him. All this points toward casting a woman much younger than Caesar as Calphurnia, a woman before whom he must maintain his virility, towards whom he is both authoritative and indulgent, and someone, however dear to him she may be, with whom he does not share his deepest thoughts and feelings. This casting choice seems to be both adequate psychology and good theatre. After his assertion that he *will* go, she builds for him an accumulation of the fearful signs and portents which have so frightened her. He tries to mollify her, first (ll. 26-27) with a courageous fatalism and then with his logical assertion that the predictions apply to everybody. She sticks to her guns, and he tries to calm her with the often-quoted lines (ll. 32-36) about the inevitability of death. Her reply is forestalled by the entrance of the Servant.

37-56 The Servant reports the negative result of the augurers, to which Caesar *must* respond, after the previous bout with Calphurnia, with bravado. She retorts with vehemence: "Your wisdom is consumed in confidence," and then tries one last face-saving ploy, desperately pleading on her knees, echoing Portia on her knees. Caesar indulgently, and not against his will, finds he can accept this way out, so he accedes to her request.

SERVANT They would not have you to stir forth today.
Plucking the entrails of an offering forth,
They could not find a heart within the beast.

CAESAR The gods do this in shame of cowardice.
Caesar should be° a beast without a heart
If he should stay at home today for fear.
No, Caesar shall not. Danger knows full well
That Caesar is more dangerous than he.
We are two lions littered in one day,
And I the elder and more terrible,
And Caesar shall go forth.

CALPHURNIA Alas, my lord,
Your wisdom is consumed in confidence.°
Do not go forth today. Call it my fear
That keeps you in the house, and not your own.
We'll send Mark Antony to the Senate House,
And he shall say you are not well today.
Let me upon my knee prevail in this.

CAESAR Mark Antony shall say I am not well,
And for thy humor° I will stay at home.

Enter DECIUS.

Here's Decius Brutus, he shall tell them so.

DECIUS Caesar, all hail! Good morrow, worthy Caesar;
I come to fetch° you to the Senate House.

CAESAR And you are come in very happy time°
To bear my greeting to the senators
And tell them that I will not come today.
Cannot, is false; and that I dare not, falser.
I will not come today; tell them so, Decius.

CALPHURNIA Say he is sick.

CAESAR Shall Caesar send a lie?
Have I in conquest stretched mine arm so far
To be afeard to tell greybeards the truth?
Decius, go tell them Caesar will not come.

would certainly be

i.e., an excessive and foolish confidence

whim, caprice

escort

at a very favorable moment

57-82 At this precise moment, in the way things happen in this play, Decius Brutus makes his brisk and cheerful entrance. Caesar blandly returns his cheerful tone, and in the midst of line 62, switches to a firmly determined announcement, ending cavalierly with, "Tell them so, Decius." Calphurnia puts in, "Tell them he is sick," as if to ameliorate Caesar's imperiousness. Caesar will have none of this, in the spirit of "Never apologize; never explain," but when Decius asks for help in explaining this to the Senate, inwardly hoping to find a way out of his dilemma, Caesar comes off his high horse and deigns to explain that he is indulging his wife, because of her dream. We can only assume that, earlier in the night, prior to Caesar's entrance, Calphurnia has shared this dream with Caesar, since she does not refer to it in the scene.

DECIUS Most mighty Caesar, let me know some cause,
Lest I be laughed at when I tell them so.

CAESAR The cause is in my will: I will not come;
That is enough to satisfy the Senate.
But for your private satisfaction,
Because I love you, I will let you know.
Calphurnia here, my wife, stays° me at home.
She dreamt tonight she saw my statue,°
Which, like a fountain, with an hundred spouts
Did run pure blood; and many lusty° Romans
Came smiling and did bathe their hands in it.
And these does she apply for° warnings and portents
And evils imminent; and on her knee
Hath begged that I will stay at home today.

DECIUS This dream is all amiss interpreted;
It was a vision fair and fortunate.
Your statue spouting blood in many pipes,
In which so many smiling Romans bathed,
Signifies that from you great Rome shall suck
Reviving blood, and that great men shall press
For tinctures, stains, relics, and cognizance°.
This by Calphurnia's dream is signified.

CAESAR And this way have you well expounded it.

DECIUS I have, when you have heard what I can say—
And know it now: the Senate have concluded
To give this day a crown to mighty Caesar.
If you shall send them word you will not come,
Their minds may change. Besides, it were a mock
Apt to be rendered° for some one to say,
"Break up° the Senate till another time,
When Caesar's wife shall meet° with better dreams."
If Caesar hide himself, shall they not whisper,
"Lo, Caesar is afraid"?
Pardon me, Caesar, for my dear dear love
To your proceeding° bids me tell you this;
And reason to my love is liable.°

CAESAR How foolish do your fears seem now, Calphurnia!

keeps
(trisyllabic)

vigorous, spirited

interpret as

83-107 Decius adroitly reinterprets the dream, to Caesar's satisfaction, and, at line 93, dangles the bait of a crown scheduled to be offered Caesar. This is the first mention of such a possibility since the unsuccessful events of the Lupercal, and it seems to be something Decius has invented on the spur of the moment to ensure Caesar's attendance. Decius knows his man well, for in the next breath he suggests how Caesar may be vulnerable to mockery for uxoriously being guided by Calphurnia's fears. His tactics work, and Caesar brushes his wife's concern aside and calls for his robe.

quintessences or elixirs, heraldic colors, venerated remains, heraldic emblem

scornful retort likely to be made

adjourn

(wordplay on the senses "chance upon" and "dream"—"mete" is to dream)

advancement

i.e., I have subordinated my reason to my affection for you

I am ashamèd I did yield to them.
Give me my robe,° for I will go.

Enter BRUTUS, LIGARIUS, METELLUS, CASCA, TREBONIUS, CINNA, *and* PUBLIUS.

And look where Publius is come to fetch me.

PUBLIUS Good morrow, Caesar.

CAESAR Welcome, Publius.
What, Brutus, are you stirred so early too?
Good morrow, Casca. Caius Ligarius,
Caesar was ne'er so much your enemy°
As that same ague which hath made you lean.
What is't a clock?

BRUTUS Caesar, 'tis strucken eight.

CAESAR I thank you for your pains and courtesy.

Enter ANTONY.

See, Antony, that revels long a-nights,
Is notwithstanding up. Good morrow, Antony.

ANTONY So to most noble Caesar.

CAESAR Bid them prepare° within.
I am to blame to be thus waited for.
Now Cinna, now Metellus. What, Trebonius,
I have an hour's talk in store for you;
Remember that you call on me today;
Be near me, that I may remember you.

TREBONIUS Caesar, I will. *[Aside]* And so near will I be,
That your best friends shall wish I had been further.

CAESAR Good friends, go in and taste some wine with me,
And we, like friends, will straightway go together.

BRUTUS *[Aside]* That every like is not the same°, O Caesar,
The heart of Brutus earns° to think upon. *Exeunt.*

toga

108-119 The conspirators arrive in a body, preceded by Publius, not part of the plot, whom they have apparently met at the door. The order of their entrance is indicated, not so much by the list in the stage directions, as by the order in which Caesar greets them. The stage directions do not list Cassius among those present, in spite of his line in the preceding scene, "Nay, we will all of us be there to fetch him." In performance, Cassius is usually present, and often Caesar "accidentally" fails to include him in his jaunty greetings. Antony, after an absence from the play, is reintroduced in his role as "playboy."

(Ligarius had supported Pompey against Caesar in the Civil War)

i.e., the wine (see line 126)

120-128 In performance, Caesar is helped into his robe—probably around line 120—after the more important conspirators have been established. Trebonius' sinister aside may also be used to help cover the "robe" business. Brutus's aside surely covers the trooping off of Caesar and the group of senators and seems to call for direct speech to the audience as the others leave. Brutus can turn and join the end of the group after his speech, leaving with them.

(Brutus is playing on the distinction between similarity and identity)

grieves

Scene iii *Enter* Artemidorus, *[reading a paper].*

Artemidorus "Caesar, beware of Brutus; take heed of Cassius; come not near Casca; have an eye to Cinna; trust not Trebonius; mark well Metellus Cimber; Decius Brutus loves thee not; thou hast wronged Caius Ligarius. There is but one mind in all these men, and it is bent° against Caesar. If thou beest not immortal, look about you. Security° gives way to° conspiracy. The mighty gods defend thee!

Thy lover°, ARTEMIDORUS."

Here will I stand till Caesar pass along,
And as a suitor will I give him this.
My heart laments that virtue cannot live
Out of the teeth of emulation.°
If thou read this, O Caesar, thou mayest live;
If not, the Fates with traitors do contrive.° *Exit.*

Scene iv *Enter* Portia *and* Lucius.

Portia I prithee, boy. Run to the Senate House;
Stay not to answer me, but get thee gone.
Why dost thou stay?

Lucius To know my errand, madam.

Portia I would have had thee there and here again
Ere I can tell thee what thou shouldst do there.
[Aside] O constancy°, be strong upon my side,
Set a huge mountain 'tween my heart and tongue.
I have a man's mind, but a woman's might.
How hard it is for women to keep counsel!°
—Art thou here yet?

Lucius Madam, what should I do?
Run to the Capitol, and nothing else?
And so return to you, and nothing else?

Portia Yes, bring me word, boy, if thy Lord look well,
For he went sickly forth; and take good note
What Caesar doth, what suitors press to him.
Hark, boy, what noise is that?

Lucius I hear none, madam.

directed

lack of care, overconfidence opens the path to

devoted friend

beyond the biting fangs of envious rivalry

conspire

fortitude, self-control

preserve secrecy

Stage Direction: The action, as Artemidorus reviews his letter, now moves to the street and remains there until the move to "the Capitol" early in Act III, Sc. i. There is a gradual building of people and bustle from Artemidorus, in soliloquy, through to the ceremonies of Caesar's entrance.

1-14 Artemidorus' letter lists the very men we have just seen surrounding Caesar. The play does not deal with how he knows about the conspiracy; it is sufficient for the author's building of suspense that he does so. "Here will I stand till Caesar pass along," is another example of Shakespeare's deft poetic scene setting. We may have wondered *who* this person is, but as soon as the letter defines his *purpose*, Shakespeare lets us know *where* he is. Although there is an *exit* indicated here, and a new scene number appears in the text for the Portia/Lucius scene, we must remember that there was no interruption in the stage action at these scene ends. In performance, there is every reason to suppose that from the end of Artemidorus' speech till Caesar's entrance, the crowd of onlookers increases in number. Others could come and take their places along Caesar's route, jostling for position, before Portia and Lucius enter.

Act II, Scene iv: This scene is often cut in performance, so that the play can move directly to Caesar's entrance. What is it meant to accomplish? It reminds us of Portia and "pads out" her function. It reminds us that Brutus failed to come back and share the knowledge of the conspiracy with her. It lets us know Portia guesses Brutus' purpose, and it seems to suggest that she supports that purpose. None of this really contributes in any essential way to the action of the play.

1-20 Portia seems to be in some confusion of mind, since she tries to send Lucius on an errand without defining it. Her aside prays for self-control and the ability to keep a secret, implying that she has guessed what it is. When Lucius wants to know what he is supposed to do, she seems at first to devise a fake errand (whether Brutus looks well) but her request about what suitors press near Caesar is closer to the mark. She seems, in the bustle and fray she hears, to have a premonition, for Lucius seems not to hear the same thing.

PORTIA Prithee listen well.
I heard a bustling rumor° like a fray,°
And the wind brings it from the Capitol.

LUCIUS Sooth° madam, I hear nothing.

Enter the SOOTHSAYER.

PORTIA Come hither, fellow. Which way hast thou been?

SOOTHSAYER At mine own house, good lady.

PORTIA What is't a clock?

SOOTHSAYER About the ninth hour, lady.

PORTIA Is Caesar yet gone to the Capitol?

SOOTHSAYER Madam, not yet. I go to take my stand,
To see him pass on to the Capitol.

PORTIA Thou hast some suit to Caesar, hast thou not?

SOOTHSAYER That I have, lady, if it will please Caesar
To be so good to Caesar as to hear me.
I shall beseech him to befriend himself.

PORTIA Why, know'st thou any harm's intended towards him?

SOOTHSAYER None that I know will be, much that I fear may chance.°
Good morrow to you. Here the street is narrow.
The throng that follows Caesar at the heels,
Of senators, of praetors,° common suitors,
Will crowd a feeble man almost to death.
I'll get me to a place more void,° and there
Speak to great Caesar as he comes along. *Exit.*

PORTIA *[Aside]* I must go in. Ay me, how weak a thing
The heart of woman is! O Brutus,
The heavens speed thee° in thine enterprise.
Sure the boy heard me. Brutus hath a suit
That Caesar will not grant. O I grow faint.
—Run, Lucius, and commend me to° my lord;
Say I am merry.° Come to me again,
And bring me word what he doth say to thee.

Exeunt [at different doors].

confused and agitated noise
fight

in sooth, truly

20-38 As part of the assembling crowd, the Soothsayer enters. Portia hails him as he passes by. Her question about the time has to do with finding out how soon the Senate's meeting is to begin, and it also fixes the time for the audience. She is alerted by the man's remark about befriending Caesar. The Soothsayer makes the interesting comment that he doesn't know of any harm that *will be*, but that he fears what may *chance*. He then excuses himself to find a better vantage point.

happen

high-ranking magistrates

more empty

39-46 Portia, pleading faintness, justifes her exit—and then, near the end of the scene, reveals that she guesses at and sympathizes with Brutus' "enterprise." The suggestion, "Sure the boy heard me," in an aside is very odd indeed, almost challenging the play's own stage conventions. Then she covers by sending Lucius away on a pretext, but really in order that he may bring back news. She goes in again, for surely the author cannot have her around during the assassination.

make you successful

remember me kindly (a polite formula)

in good spirits

ACT III

Scene i *Flourish. Enter* Caesar, Brutus, Cassius, Casca, Decius, Metellus, Trebonius, Cinna, Antony, Lepidus, Artemidorus, Publius, [Popilius,] *and the* Soothsayer.

Caesar The ides of March are come.

Soothsayer Ay, Caesar, but not gone.

Artemidorus Hail, Caesar! Read this schedule.°

Decius Trebonius doth desire you to o'erread,
At your best leisure, this his humble suit.

Artemidorus O Caesar, read mine first; for mine's a suit
That touches° Caesar nearer. Read it, great Caesar.

Caesar What touches us ourself shall be last served.°

Artemidorus Delay not, Caesar, read it instantly.

Caesar What, is the fellow mad?

Publius Sirrah,° give place.°

Cassius What, urge you your petitions in the street?
Come to the Capitol.

[Caesar *enters the Capitol, the rest following.*]

Brutus What said Popilius Lena?

Cassius He wished today our enterprise might thrive.
I fear our purpose is discoverèd.

Brutus Look how he makes to° Caesar. Mark him.

Cassius Casca, be sudden°, for we fear prevention.°
Brutus, what shall be done? If this be known,
Cassius or Caesar never shall turn back°,
For I will slay myself.

Brutus Cassius, be constant.°
Popilius Lena speaks not of our purposes;
For look, he smiles, and Caesar doth not change.°

Stage Directions Remember that the action on the Elizabethan stage was continuous, and that the "scene setting" has already been done by Artemidorus and the Soothsayer. Although Lucius was unable to hear the bustle and fray of which Portia spoke, there is surely a goodly amount of bustle and fray, along with the "flourish" of trumpets, as Caesar enters. In performance, along with those listed as entering, one is likely to see soldiers with banners, guards to hold back the crowd, the Roman mob (since they are already on the company payroll and might as well be on the stage as in the dressing room), and as lively a stage picture as the management can muster.

document, paper

1-13 Accompanied by whatever guards to hold back the crowd and whatever press of onlookers the production provides, Caesar enters, surrounded by the senatorial conspirators who have come to escort him and to prevent anyone else from coming near him. A useful staging of this scene is to have the crowd and guards form a kind of "living curtain" across the front of the stage (downstage), so that when the stage direction tells us, "Caesar enters the Capitol, the rest following," the guards part the crowd at the center, pushing them offstage, as Caesar and his group cross upstage, with Caesar taking his place in the chair of state which has been placed for him behind the cover of the crowd which till now has filled the stage. When Caesar enters, however, the crowd is still across the stage. Probably as he reaches the center, before turning to go "to the Capitol," he sees the Soothsayer at the edge of the crowd and addresses him. The procession stops to wait for this exchange, and before it can move again, Artemidorus thrusts himself forward, holding out his paper. Before Caesar can respond, Decius intervenes. It is for just this sort of emergency that the conspirators have surrounded Caesar. As Artemidorus persists, the innocent Publius intervenes, along with Cassius, and, no doubt with the help of soldiers, Artemidorus is hustled off. Then comes the move up, during which Popilius Lena, another uninvolved senator, must be seen to mutter something in passing to Cassius and then move up to walk with Caesar to the chair of state. As part of the general move, Brutus comes to beside Cassius, and they remain downstage.

concerns

attended to

a colloquial form of "sir" (contemptuous) get out of the way

advances toward

swift being forestalled

i.e., return home alive

15-26 This sequence between Brutus and Cassius seems clearly meant to be spoken "aside," as Caesar and the senators gather upstage in the "Capitol," with Popilius Lena moving toward Caesar when the lines

resolute

i.e., change the expression on his face

CASSIUS Trebonius knows his time; for look you, Brutus,
He draws Mark Antony out of the way.

[Exeunt ANTONY *and* TREBONIUS.*]*

DECIUS Where is Metellus Cimber? Let him go
And presently° prefer° his suit to Caesar.

BRUTUS He is addressed.° Press near and second him.

CINNA Casca, you are the first that rears your hand.

CAESAR Are we all ready? What is now amiss
That Caesar and his Senate must redress?

METELLUS Most high, most mighty, and most puissant° Caesar,
Metellus Cimber throws before thy seat
An humble heart.

CAESAR I must prevent° thee, Cimber.
These couchings° and these lowly courtesies°
Might fire the blood of ordinary men
And turn preordinance and first decree°
Into the law of children.° Be not fond°
To think that Caesar bears such rebel blood°
That will be thawed° from the true° quality
With that which melteth fools; I mean sweet words,
Low-crookèd°curtsies, and base spaniel fawning.°
Thy brother by decree is banishèd.
If thou dost bend and pray and fawn for him,
I spurn thee like a cur out of my way.
Know, Caesar doth not wrong, nor without cause
Will he be satisfied.

METELLUS Is there no voice more worthy than my own
To sound more sweetly in great Caesar's ear
For the repealing° of my banished brother?

BRUTUS I kiss thy hand, but not in flattery, Caesar;
Desiring thee that Publius Cimber may
Have an immediate freedom of repeal.°

CAESAR What, Brutus?

indicate. Also within these lines, as indicated, Trebonius invents a pretext to take Antony offstage. If the production has made use of guards and soldiers, as suggested above, it is easy to get them off (so they aren't around to protect Caesar during the assassination) as they clear the crowd away during the move "to the Capitol."

at once present

ready

27-29 Decius, who must have been preoccupied with watching Antony leave or some other necessary function, comes down at this point to ask, "aside," about Metellus Cimber. Brutus, facing up toward Caesar, tells him Cimber is "on cue", and as Brutus, Cassius, and Decius move up to join the group around Caesar, Cinna moves near to Casca and, aside, reminds him of their plan of action. This sequence, from the beginning of the scene till now, is one of the most complex staging problems Shakespeare poses a director, but if one takes one's cue from the author's stage directions as implied in the dialogue, one cannot go far wrong.

powerful

forestall

bowings humble obeisances

i.e., the preordained natural laws of the Universe, decreed from the beginning of time

childishly capricious order so foolish as

has such a rebellious disposition

(Caesar's blood is icy) proper

bent low currying favor like a dog

recalling from banishment

permission to be recalled from exile

30-75 Caesar, standing or sitting (if the director employs a chair of state), calls the Senate to order. As planned, Metellus Cimber steps in to begin his petition. The idea seems to be that the conspirators will one by one kneel around Caesar in support of Cimber's petition and kill Caesar after he is surrounded. Caesar interrupts Cimber, rejecting his fawning beginning and haughtily denying Cimber's suit to repeal the banishment of his brother. When Cimber asks for support, Brutus, to Caesar's surprise, joins in, followed by Cassius. This produces from Caesar a speech imperiously comparing himself with the Northern Star, as a constant among men. One is reminded, as one hears the speech, of fate and destiny as governed by the stars, and this sense of unleashed, tragic pride is furthered, after Cinna adds his voice, by Caesar's line comparing himself with "Olympus." There is a long musical build here, too, all the way from line 35, "I must prevent thee, Cimber," through to Casca's "Speak hands for me!" Pitch and tension rise as suspense builds for what the audience knows is coming, until Casca's shout and his blow climax this section and begin the almost ritual slaying.

CASSIUS Pardon, Caesar; Caesar, pardon.
As low as to thy foot doth Cassius fall
To beg enfranchisement for Publius Cimber.

CAESAR I could be well moved, if I were as you;
If I could pray to move,° prayers would move me.
But I am constant as the Northern Star,°
Of whose true-fixed and resting° quality
There is no fellow° in the firmament.
The skies are painted° with unnumb'red sparks,
They are all fire, and every one doth shine;
But there's but one in all doth hold his place.
So in the world: 'tis furnished well with men,
And men are flesh and blood, and apprehensive;°
Yet in the number I do know but one
That unassailable holds on his rank,°
Unshaked of motion;° and that I am he,
Let me a little show it, even in this:
That I was constant° Cimber should be banished,
And constant do remain to keep him so.

CINNA O Caesar—

CAESAR Hence! Wilt thou lift up Olympus?°

DECIUS Great Caesar—

CAESAR Doth not Brutus bootless° kneel?

CASCA Speak hands for me! *They stab* CAESAR.

CAESAR Et tu, Brutè?°— Then fall, Caesar. *Dies.*

CINNA Liberty! Freedom! Tyranny is dead!
Run hence, proclaim, cry it about the streets.

CASSIUS Some to the common pulpits,° and cry out,
"Liberty, freedom, and enfranchisement!"

BRUTUS People and senators, be not affrighted.
Fly not; stand still. Ambition's debt is paid.°

CASCA Go to the pulpit, Brutus.

DECIUS And Cassius too.

BRUTUS Where's Publius?

i.e., prevail upon others through strong entreaty

the polestar by which mariners steer

immovable

equal

adorned

capable of apprehending

keeps his position

unmoved by any influences

resolute

a mountain in Greece thought to be the home of the gods

in vain

and thou, Brutus

platforms or stages from which public speeches were delivered

i.e., Caesar has received his just deserts for his ambition

77 No lines are given until Caesar's dying words. Kemble's 1817 performance of the play offered the assassination, as the critic Tieck put it, "like the most formal ballet." After being struck by Casca, Caesar turned to the right, receiving a second blow from another enemy, staggered back in the other direction, and so on, staggering across the stage several times, stabbed by the conspirators, who remained quietly standing, till receiving his death blow from Brutus. Another 19th Century production has all the killers except Brutus and Cassius rush on Caesar at once to stab him. Then Cassius pulled him from the throne, stabbed him, and threw him over to Brutus, who then finished him off. The text seems to suggest silence until after Caesar's "Et tu, Brute?—Then fall, Caesar." Phelps' production, in 1846, played all this in silence, until Caesar fell, at which there was a great outcry in panic from the bystanders.

78-99 This seems to be borne out by the text as well, for at line 78, Cinna breaks out with shouts of, "Liberty," etc., which could well be the cue for a general outcry. Cassius includes the outside world, telling them to cry out, "Liberty, freedom, and enfranchisement," in the common pulpits. Brutus addresses, "People and senators," in his next line, which indicates even more clearly the presence of others who are "affrighted." The tempo and pressure, and probably the noise from outside, continue through the sending away of Publius, Metellus' warning, and the return of Trebonius.

CINNA Here, quite confounded with this mutiny.°

METELLUS Stand fast together, lest some friend of Caesar's
Should chance—

BRUTUS Talk not of standing.° Publius, good cheer,
There is no harm intended to your person,
Nor to no Roman else. So tell them, Publius.

CASSIUS And leave us, Publius, lest that the people,
Rushing on us, should do your age some mischief.

BRUTUS Do so, and let no man abide° this deed
But we the doers.

Enter TREBONIUS.

CASSIUS Where is Antony?

TREBONIUS Fled to his house amazed.°
Men, wives, and children stare, cry out, and run,
As° it were doomsday.

BRUTUS Fates, we will know your pleasures.
That we shall die, we know; 'tis but the time
And drawing days out,° that men stand upon.°

CASCA Why, he that cuts off twenty years of life
Cuts off so many years of fearing death.

BRUTUS Grant that, and then is death a benefit.
So are we Caesar's friends, that have abridged
His time of fearing death. Stoop, Romans, stoop,
And let us bathe our hands in Caesar's blood
Up to the elbows, and besmear our swords.
Then walk we forth, even to the market place, °
And waving our red weapons o'er our heads,
Let's all cry, "Peace, freedom, and liberty!"

CASSIUS Stoop then, and wash. How many ages hence
Shall this our lofty scene be acted over,
In states unborn and accents yet unknown!

BRUTUS How many times shall Caesar bleed in sport?°

stunned by this uproar

i.e., standing fast together

pay the penalty for

astounded

as if

prolonging life attach importance to

i.e., the Roman Forum

i.e., in a play

99-122 There is a quality of fervent release and an almost religious dedication apparent in the speeches of Brutus, beginning with, "Fates, we will know your pleasures." The deed is done, the die is cast, the inevitable is set in motion. Casca seconds him in this fervor. Out of this collective "high" comes Brutus's grotesque but dedicated urging that they "stoop" and "bathe" up to the elbows and smear their swords with Caesar's blood. In the 19th Century most productions decorously omitted this barbarity, and there are certainly practical theatrical reasons for doing so. In production, how is the blood to get there? A modern solution: one of the less prominent conspirators from the entrance palms a "blood-soaked" sponge, and from behind the obstacle of Caesar's body, they all get some blood on their hands and weapons as they kneel. In Roman costume, the white togas present the next serious problem: the actors *must* hold their hands out or up away from their sides if their costumes are not to be soiled by the stage blood. Until very recently, no convincing coloring matter for stage blood was available which came fully clean, so, during a run, the sides of the togas were apt to become gradually pinker and pinker. During the intensity of playing, even the most precise of actors is apt to become careless, and people do brush against one another. Still, the effect is very well worth it. From the

That now on Pompey's basis lies along°
No worthier than the dust!

CASSIUS So oft as that shall be,
So often shall the knot° of us be called
The men that gave their country liberty.

DECIUS What, shall we forth?

CASSIUS Ay, every man away.
Brutus shall lead, and we will grace° his heels
With the most boldest and best hearts of Rome.

Enter a SERVANT.

BRUTUS Soft°, who comes here? A friend of Antony's.

SERVANT Thus, Brutus, did my master bid me kneel;
Thus did Mark Antony bid me fall down;
And being prostrate, thus he bade me say:
Brutus is noble, wise, valiant, and honest;°
Caesar was mighty, bold, royal, and loving.
Say, I love Brutus and I honor him;
Say, I feared Caesar, honored him, and loved him.
If Brutus will vouchsafe that Antony
May safely come to him, and be resolved°
How Caesar hath deserved to lie in death,
Mark Antony shall not love Caesar dead
So well as Brutus living; but will follow
The fortunes and affairs of noble Brutus
Thorough° the hazards of this untrod state°
With all true faith. So says my master Antony.

BRUTUS Thy master is a wise and valiant Roman;
I never thought him worse.
Tell him, so please him come° unto this place,
He shall be satisfied;° and by my honor
Depart untouched.

SERVANT I'll fetch him presently.° *Exit* SERVANT.

BRUTUS I know that we shall have him well to friend.°

CASSIUS I wish we may. But yet have I a mind

lies stretched out at the pedestal of Pompey's statue

closely bound group

moment the killers rise, they must hold their bloody swords and hands aloft or out, and when Antony comes in, this barbaric sight greets him. He must shake their bloody hands, and Caesar's blood will still be on his hands after they leave him alone with the body. The effect is *essential* if the author's intention is to be realized. Another theatrical footnote: during a run, the actors will tend to use less and less of the sticky and inhibiting stage blood, and they must be encouraged not to be stingy with it just for the sake of the cleaning bill.

do honor to

wait a moment (a common Elizabethan interjection)

honorable

have his doubts cleared up

(dissyllabic variant of "through") new and uncertain state of affairs

if it should please him to come

have full information

at once

for a friend

123-147 At the height of the conspirators' post-mortem fervor, everything stops, as Brutus, looking off, sees Antony's Servant approach. The stage freezes as he enters, kneels, and speaks. This moment is an example of how Shakespeare from time to time places a task of great importance in the hands of a small-part actor. The Servant must speak clearly, carefully, and above all, *neutrally*, in order not to rouse the ire of the conspirators while at the same time not sounding fawningly insincere. Indeed, his task is a foretaste of what Antony's will be when he enters. His message, of course, is to ask for (1) a safe conduct for his master, in order that Antony may (2) be given reasons for the conspirators' action. Brutus graciously acknowledges Antony's status. Note that line 140 is a short line, with only three major stresses instead of five. Such short lines usually indicate some "time-out" for physical action. Perhaps Brutus takes a moment to consider; perhaps he looks at Cassius to say, "You may not like this, but it's the right thing to do." Perhaps something else was intended; but at short lines, the author is always trying to tell us something. The servant gravely departs, and Brutus, almost as if forestalling any objection, firmly states his position on Antony. Cassius makes his uneasiness clear.

That fears him much; and my misgiving still
Falls shrewdly to the purpose.°

Enter ANTONY.

BRUTUS But here comes Antony. Welcome, Mark Antony.

ANTONY O mighty Caesar! Dost thou lie so low?
Are all thy conquests, glories, triumphs, spoils,
Shrunk to this little measure? Fare thee well.
I know not, gentlemen, what you intend,
Who else must be let blood°, who else is rank.°
If I myself, there is no hour so fit
As Caesar's death's hour; nor no instrument
Of half that worth as those your swords, made rich
With the most noble blood of all this world.
I do beseech ye, if you bear me hard,°
Now, whilst your purpled hands do reek and smoke,
Fulfil your pleasure. Live° a thousand years,
I shall not find myself so apt to die.
No place will please me so, no mean° of death,
As here by Caesar, and by you cut off,
The choice and master spirits of this age.

BRUTUS O Antony! Beg not your death of us.
Though now we must appear bloody and cruel,
As by our hands and this our present act
You see we do; yet see you but our hands,
And this the bleeding business they have done.
Our hearts you see not; they are pitiful;°
And pity to the general wrong of Rome—
As fire drives out fire, so pity pity—
Hath done this deed on Caesar. For your part,
To you our swords have leaden° points, Mark Antony.
Our arms in strength of malice,° and our hearts
Of brothers' temper,° do receive you in
With all kind love, good thoughts, and reverence.

CASSIUS Your voice° shall be as strong as any man's
In the disposing of new dignities.°

BRUTUS Only be patient till we have appeased

always turns out to be unpleasantly near the truth

148-151 Antony enters, and that Cassius' previous line is a short one clearly indicates that they turn in silence to look where he approaches. Brutus speaks just before Antony appears (since he can't say "here comes Antony" after he has arrived) and greets him formally on his entrance. Antony's attention is riveted on the corpse of Caesar, and he probably goes straight to the body. His words are oddly non-committal—"Has it all come to this? Goodbye." We will learn only from the later soliloquy with what effort he is holding himself in.

(medical bloodletting as a euphemism for "putting to death") corrupt, festering/overgrown, luxuriant

152-164 Only at "I know not, gentlemen . . ." does he at last look at Caesar's killers. His tone at first seems even and careful, as he spells out "let blood" and "rank," but by "If I myself . . ." courage and pride assert themselves. From "I do beseech ye . ." to the end of the speech, a ringing sincerity and a note of proud challenge seem to dominate, but he is careful to end with what seems to be a chivalrous acknowledgement of their standing. Perhaps already in his head the bitter ironies of the later "honorable men" are forming, but he can allow no note of sarcasm to enter here. His straightforward and honest handling of these critical first moments impresses Brutus, but for the audience this scene creates suspense about how Antony is going to take this event. In the theatre, the actors must always remember that the characters haven't read the play, and they must play the play, even this one, as if the audience hasn't read it either.

have a grudge against me

if I should live

means

165-184 Brutus, taking upon himself the role of spokesman for the conspirators, assures Antony both of their sincerity and of his own safety. He speaks with earnestness as he assures Antony of their regard. Cassius joins Brutus in receiving Antony peacefully, almost as a cue to the others that he intends to follow Brutus's lead, but his remark about "'the disposing of new dignities" is a practical, and not idealistic, look toward the future. Brutus quickly assures Antony that, after the people have been "appeased," reasons will be given him for Caesar's death, and the actor playing Antony can certainly imagine that the idea of finding a way to speak to the people occurs to him here. He gravely accepts Brutus's assurances.

full of pity

blunt

i.e., the conspirators appear to express strong enmity

of a brotherly disposition

vote, opinion

dispensing patronage

The multitude, beside themselves with fear,
And then we will deliver° you the cause
Why I, that did love Caesar when I struck him,
Have thus proceeded.

ANTONY I doubt not of your wisdom.
Let each man render me his bloody hand.
First, Marcus Brutus, will I shake with you;
Next, Caius Cassius, do I take your hand;
Now, Decius Brutus, yours; now yours, Metellus;
Yours, Cinna; and, my valiant° Casca, yours.
Though last, not least in love, yours, good Trebonius.
Gentlemen all—alas, what shall I say?
My credit° now stands on such slippery ground
That one of two bad ways you must conceit° me,
Either a coward or a flatterer.
That I did love thee, Caesar, O 'tis true.
If then thy spirit look upon us now,
Shall it not grieve thee dearer° than thy death
To see thy Antony making his peace,
Shaking the bloody fingers of thy foes,
Most noble, in the presence of thy corse?°
Had I as many eyes as thou hast wounds,
Weeping as fast as they stream forth thy blood,
It would become me better than to close°
In terms of friendship with thine enemies.
Pardon me, Julius! Here wast thou bayed,° brave hart;°
Here didst thou fall; and here thy hunters stand,
Signed in thy spoil° and crimsoned in thy lethe.°
O world, thou wast the forest to this hart,
And this indeed, O world, the heart of thee!
How like a deer, strucken° by many princes,
Dost thou here lie!

CASSIUS Mark Antony—

ANTONY Pardon me, Caius Cassius.
The enemies of Caesar shall say this;
Then, in a friend, it is cold modesty.°

CASSIUS I blame you not for praising Caesar so,
But what compact° mean you to have with us?

report to

185-190 Now comes the important and solemn moment where Antony takes each of them by the bloody hand, and, seeming to assure them of his acceptance, actually marks each of them down for vengeance. Here the business of Caesar's blood being on each hand and transferred to Antony's hand has a powerful theatrical effectiveness.

(an ironical allusion to Casca's cowardly blow to Caesar from behind)

credibility

conceive of

191-211 Having finished making his rounds to clasp their hands, one by one, he now stands among them, his hands bloodied too. The question he asks now, having so far earned his own survival—what can they think of him—is the audience's question as well. What kind of person is this? Subtext for the actor playing Antony will probably have to do with, "How is Antony going to skate on this thin ice with any credibility? By admitting what is true—the feeling for Caesar—and, like the accomplished liar and tactician he is, adapting the truth, as best he can, to the service of the impression he must create." Caesar's blood on his hands leads him to confront Caesar's body, and Antony "uses" (in actors' terminology) his real feelings now to convince everyone of his entire sincerity, asking the dead Caesar's corpse to forgive him—in terms not so different from those he will use when he is alone with the body—and finishing with an outpouring of grief-stricken praise.

more keenly

corpse

make an agreement

brought to bay (pun on *heart-hart,* a deer)

marked with the blood of your slaughter the river of forgetfulness in Hades

struck down

211-232 Cassius interrupts what indeed has begun to sound as if it might go on forever, and Antony dares, so it seems, to assert his rights as Caesar's friend with some asperity. Cassius cuts right through to the real question: "What are we supposed to do about you?" Antony, almost humbly, acknowledges his acceptance of them, his only proviso being that, as Brutus has already offered, they make clear to him why they have acted. Only after Brutus righteously reaffirms this does Antony, surely with great humilty, dare to ask for the right to "speak in the order of his funeral." The actor playing Antony must surely let no whiff of his real purpose show here, and Brutus, in the grip of his own magnanimity, firmly grants his request.

moderation

agreement, accord

Will you be pricked in number of our° friends,
Or shall we on,° and not depend on you?

ANTONY Therefore I took your hands, but was indeed
Swayed from the point by looking down on Caesar.
Friends am I with you all, and love you all,
Upon this hope, that you shall give me reasons
Why and wherein Caesar was dangerous.

BRUTUS Or else were this a savage spectacle.
Our reasons are so full of good regard°
That were you, Antony, the son of Caesar,
You should be satisfied.

ANTONY That's all I seek,
And am moreover suitor that I may
Produce° his body to the market place,
And in the pulpit, as becomes a friend,
Speak in the order of his funeral.°

BRUTUS You shall, Mark Antony.

CASSIUS Brutus, a word with you.
[Aside to BRUTUS*]* You know not what you do. Do not consent
That Antony speak in his funeral.
Know you how much the people may be moved
By that which he will utter?

BRUTUS *[Aside to* CASSIUS*]* By your pardon—
I will myself into the pulpit first,
And show the reason of our Caesar's death.
What Antony shall speak, I will protest °
He speaks by leave and by permission;
And that we are contented Caesar shall
Have all true° rites and lawful ceremonies,
It shall advantage° more than do us wrong.

CASSIUS *[Aside to* BRUTUS*]* I know not what may fall;° I like it not.

BRUTUS Mark Antony, here, take you Caesar's body.
You shall not in your funeral speech blame us,
But speak all good you can devise of Caesar,
And say you do't by our permission.
Else shall you not have any hand at all

marked down among

i.e., go on, proceed

so convincingly worthy

bring forward

his funeral ceremonies

232-254: Cassius is instantly alerted to the danger of Antony's speaking and quickly breaks in. Note that his interruption comes within the same line of verse as Brutus's granting of the request. "You know not what you do," is as bluntly put as anyone has dared to speak to Brutus in the play, and that choice of words suggests the energy and conviction with which Cassius must deliver his warning when he takes Brutus aside. Brutus spells out the course he will take to avoid whatever danger exists and asserts, stubbornly, that Antony's presence there will "advantage more than do us wrong." *The First Folio* does not include the stage direction at line 233: "Aside to Brutus" nor the next two "Aside" directions. They seem entirely justified, however, except that a better staging might be that after "more than do us wrong" (l. 243) Brutus should walk back to Antony, leaving Cassius to say, "I know not what may fall, I like it not," aside, to himself. To Antony, Brutus sternly puts the terms under which Antony will be allowed to speak, and Antony humbly accepts them. Brutus and the conspirators leave, and it makes an effective exit if, as Brutus earlier suggested, they do indeed leave with their "red weapons" held aloft, in defiant pride.

proclaim

due and proper

benefit

befall

About his funeral. And you shall speak
In the same pulpit whereto I am going,
After my speech is ended.

ANTONY Be it so;
I do desire no more.

BRUTUS Prepare the body then, and follow us.

Exeunt. ANTONY *remains.*

ANTONY O pardon me, thou bleeding piece of earth,
That I am meek and gentle with these butchers.
Thou art the ruins of the noblest man
That ever livèd in the tide of times.°
Woe to the hand that shed this costly° blood!
Over thy wounds now do I prophesy
(Which like dumb mouths do ope their ruby lips
To beg the voice and utterance of my tongue),
A curse shall light° upon the limbs of men;
Domestic fury and fierce civil strife
Shall cumber° all the parts of Italy;
Blood and destruction shall be so in use,°
And dreadful objects° so familiar,
That mothers shall but smile when they behold
Their infants quartered with the hands of war,
All pity choked with custom of fell deeds;°
And Caesar's spirit, ranging° for revenge,
With Atè° by his side come hot from hell,
Shall in these confines° with a monarch's voice
Cry "Havoc!"° and let slip° the dogs of war,
That° this foul° deed shall smell above the earth
With carrion men,° groaning for burial.

Enter OCTAVIO'S SERVANT.

You serve Octavius Caesar, do you not?

SERVANT I do, Mark Antony.

ANTONY Caesar did write for him to come to Rome.

SERVANT He did receive his letters and is coming,

course of history

(wordplay on dear and valuable and dearly bought, grievous)

alight

burden

customary

sights

being accustomed to savage and cruel acts

roving about

(Greek goddess of discord and vengeance)

boundaries

a military order for unlimited slaughter unleash

so that morally corrupt/stinking

i.e., corpses beginning to decay

255-276: Now Antony is free to give vent to his true feelings. "Butchers," he calls them, as he contemplates the "bleeding piece of earth" which is "the ruins of the noblest man." The first four lines of the speech are an apology to the corpse. At "Woe to the hand..." there is a vow of vengeance, and at line 260 the prophesy of vengeance begins a long build, or *crescendo*, extending from "Over thy wounds," all the way to "Cry 'Havoc!' " In the course of the prophesy, or curse, the speaker goes from the wounds of the corpse over which he kneels up to "all the parts of Italy," and then to "Caesar's spirit, ranging for revenge," no doubt in the air, from which its "monarch's voice" cries out. The rest of that line ("and let slip the dogs of war") brings us down from the long build, so that the music of the last two lines can be low in pitch and volume, bringing the speech full circle from its beginning, back to "this foul deed" before which Antony kneels.

277-298: The entrance of Octavius' Servant breaks the spell cast by the powerful soliloquy. Antony sees someone enter; is this the approach of danger? But he recognizes the man, and he remembers that Caesar had sent for Octavius. The Servant tries to deliver his message, but breaks off in grief at Caesar's death. Has he just perceived the body? Much rehearsal time can be wasted trying to determine the exact positions of the characters to bring about this discovery. But suppose in the moment of entering, as Antony is recognising who the Servant is, the Servant is seeing the body and is immediate-

And bid me say to you by word of mouth—
O Caesar!

ANTONY Thy heart is big°; get thee apart and weep.
Passion° I see is catching, for mine eyes,
Seeing those beads of sorrow stand in thine,
Began to water. Is thy master coming?

SERVANT He lies tonight within seven leagues of Rome.

ANTONY Post° back with speed, and tell him what hath chanced.
Here is a mourning Rome, a dangerous Rome,
No Rome° of safety for Octavius yet;
Hie° hence and tell him so. Yet stay awhile;
Thou shalt not back till I have borne this corse
Into the market place. There shall I try,°
In my oration, how the people take
The cruel issue° of these bloody men;
According to the which° thou shalt discourse
To young Octavius of the state of things.
Lend me your hand. *Exeunt [with* CAESAR's *body].*

Scene ii *Enter* BRUTUS *and* CASSIUS, *with* the PLEBEIANS.

PLEBEIANS We will be satisfied.° Let us be satisfied.

BRUTUS Then follow me, and give me audience, friends.
Cassius, go you into the other street,
And part° the numbers.
Those that will hear me speak, let 'em stay here;
Those that will follow Cassius, go with him;
And public reasons° shall be renderèd
Of Caesar's death.

FIRST PLEBEIAN I will hear Brutus speak.

SECOND PLEBEIAN I will hear Cassius, and compare their reasons
When severally° we hear them renderèd.

[Exit CASSIUS, *with some of the* PLEBEIANS.*]*
BRUTUS *goes into the pulpit.*

THIRD PLEBEIAN The noble Brutus is ascended. Silence!

ly grief-stricken. Antony asks him a question. The Servant does his best to answer but finally gives way to his emotion. No awkward staging problem exists. Often in Shakespeare actors set themselves non-existent problems and then torture themselves trying to solve them. At line 285, when both men have had time to control themselves, Antony decides to warn Octavius off, and then he realizes at line 291 that the Servant can wait to see how Antony's oration goes and inform Octavius of the result. As Antony reveals to the Servant that he plans to test the people's mood with his speech, we get the first clear indication from Antony of his intention. Note that the Servant probably has men with him, for he and Antony could scarcely be expected to get the body offstage gracefully by themselves. From Antony's entrance to find the conspirators around the body of Caesar, the play has moved into its second phase—what will Antony be able to do about the murder.

swollen with grief

strong feeling, sorrow

ride quickly, hasten

(pun on *Rome-room*)

hasten

test

the outcome of the conspirators' cruelty

i.e., the effect of my oration

Stage Directions "With the Plebeians." Four Plebeians are assignzed lines. Four plebeians do not a "mob" make. In the Joseph Mankiewicz film version of the play, James Mason as Brutus and Marlon Brando as Antony had a huge crowd to address, so that the sack of Rome after Antony's oration could be of realistic size. In the early outdoor productions of the play for the New York Shakespeare Festival, union regulations still made it possible to assemble as many extras as the theatre could afford to costume. In recent years, such massive groups have become impractical in the professional theatre, and some stylization of the "mob" has become necessary. Whatever size the mob is, the four people assigned lines can become group leaders, helping to organize and control the "ad libs" of the others around them. The lines, as given, become themes for improvization until the "ad libs" become fixed, as they must, in rehearsal.

insist on a full explanation

divide

i.e., reasons related to the public good

separately

1-10 Shakespeare gets Cassius offstage, partly to give us a sense that Rome is indeed larger than his stage can depict, but mainly to avoid having Cassius around for the two orations. Cassius would never have permitted Antony to speak without supervision, as Brutus is to allow him to do.

BRUTUS Be patient till the last.°

Romans, countrymen, and lovers°, hear me for my cause, and be silent, that you may hear. Believe me for mine honor, and have respect° to mine honor, that you may believe. Censure° me in your wisdom, and awake your senses°, that you may the better judge. If there be any in this assembly, any dear friend of Caesar's, to him I say that Brutus' love to Caesar was no less than his. If then that friend demand why Brutus rose against Caesar, this is my answer: Not that I loved Caesar less, but that I loved Rome more. Had you rather Caesar were living, and die all slaves, than that Caesar were dead, to live all free men? As Caesar loved me, I weep for him; as he was fortunate, I rejoice at it; as he was valiant, I honor him; but, as he was ambitious, I slew him. There is tears for his love; joy for his fortune; honor for his valor; and death for his ambition. Who is here so base that would be a bondman?° If any, speak; for him have I offended. Who is here so rude° that would not be a Roman? If any, speak; for him have I offended. Who is here so vile that will not love his country? If any, speak; for him have I offended. I pause for a reply.

ALL None, Brutus, none.

BRUTUS Then none have I offended. I have done no more to Caesar than you shall do° to Brutus. The question° of his death is enrolled° in the Capitol; his glory not extenuated°, wherein he was worthy; nor his offences enforced,° for which he suffered death.

Enter MARK ANTONY, *with* CAESAR'S *body.*

Here comes his body, mourned by Mark Antony, who, though he had no hand in his death, shall receive the benefit of his dying, a place° in the commonwealth, as which of you shall not? With this I depart, that, as I slew my best lover° for the good of Rome, I have the same dagger for myself when it shall please my country to need my death.

ALL Live, Brutus! live, live!

FIRST PLEBEIAN Bring him with triumph° home unto his house.

SECOND PLEBEIAN Give him a statue with his ancestors.

end of my oration
dear friends

regard judge
good sense

12-36 Shakespeare sets the Brutus oration in prose. This gives it a more pedestrian quality than verse would, although the distinction, for a listener, is very subtle. The speech is more notable for its formality and logic than for its passion. The author is "stacking the deck" for Antony, but Brutus' speech is sufficiently impressive and persuasive to convince the theatre audience, as it listens, of Brutus' sincerity and honorable intent. Indeed, that very logical and honorable sincerity is the best set-up of all for Antony's pyrotechnics which are to follow. Does Shakespeare "give the game away" with the nature of the speech he writes for Brutus? He avoids and surmounts this problem superbly! His onstage audience finds Brutus just as impressive as any Brutus could wish.

slave
ignorant, barbarous

i.e., if I offend you whole affair
i.e., recorded in the official archives understated
overly emphasized

public office
beloved, friend

Roman victory procession

37-57 Seeing Antony approach with Caesar's body borne on a bier and covered with a cloak, Brutus sets the tone for Antony as both a mourner and a beneficiary of Caesar's death. His offer to sacrifice his own life if what he has done displeases the people is sincere, and he holds his bloody dagger ready to do as they wish. The crowd hails him. Note how, as he quiets them and introduces Antony, his speech moves back into verse, simple and unadorned. With "by our permission" he thinks he has set the proper climate in which Antony is to speak, and, all alone, Brutus leaves the place convinced that he has been a great success.

THIRD PLEBEIAN Let him be Caesar.

FOURTH PLEBEIAN Caesar's better parts°
Shall be crowned in Brutus.

FIRST PLEBEIAN We'll bring him to his house with shouts and clamors.

BRUTUS My countrymen—

SECOND PLEBEIAN Peace! Silence! Brutus speaks.

FIRST PLEBEIAN Peace, ho!

BRUTUS Good countrymen, let me depart alone,
And, for my sake, stay here with Antony.
Do grace° to Caesar's corpse, and grace° his speech
Tending° to Caesar's glories, which Mark Antony,
By our permission, is allowed to make.
I do entreat you, not a man depart
Save I alone, till Antony have spoke. *Exit.*

FIRST PLEBEIAN Stay, ho! and let us hear Mark Antony.

THIRD PLEBEIAN Let him go up into the public chair;°
We'll hear him. Noble Antony, go up.

ANTONY For Brutus' sake, I am beholding° to you.

FOURTH PLEBEIAN What does he say of Brutus?

THIRD PLEBEIAN He says, for Brutus' sake
He finds himself beholding to us all.

FOURTH PLEBEIAN 'Twere best he speak no harm of Brutus here!

FIRST PLEBEIAN This Caesar was a tyrant.

THIRD PLEBEIAN Nay, that's certain.
We are blest that Rome is rid of him.

SECOND PLEBEIAN Peace! Let us hear what Antony can say.

ANTONY You gentle Romans—

ALL Peace, ho! Let us hear him.

ANTONY Friends, Romans, countrymen, lend me your ears;
I come to bury Caesar, not to praise him.

qualities

your proper respects
respect, honor
relating

58-68: Shakespeare gives us a crowd convinced by what Brutus has said. They seem willing to hear Antony, but only if he speaks well of Brutus. Note, too, that some in the crowd speak badly of Caesar even as Antony ascends the podium.

pulpit, rostrum

obliged

69-80 Antony has some trouble getting their attention, and once he does, he is careful to disclaim undue affection for Caesar—only to "bury," not to "praise." He quickly stresses that he speaks "under leave of Brutus and the rest" and uses the word "honorable" in all earnestness, both of Brutus and the

The evil that men do lives after them,
The good is oft interrèd with their bones;
So let it be with Caesar. The noble Brutus
Hath told you Caesar was ambitious.
If it were so, it was a grievous fault,
And grievously hath Caesar answered it.°
Here, under leave of Brutus and the rest—
For Brutus is an honorable man;
So are they all, all honorable men—
Come I to speak in Caesar's funeral.
He was my friend, faithful and just to me;
But Brutus says he was ambitious,
And Brutus is an honorable man.
He hath brought many captives home to Rome,
Whose ransoms did the general coffers° fill.
Did this in Caesar seem ambitious?
When that the poor have cried, Caesar hath wept.
Ambition should be made of sterner stuff,
Yet Brutus says he was ambitious;
And Brutus is an honorable man.
You all did see that on the Lupercal°
I thrice presented him a kingly crown,
Which he did thrice refuse. Was this ambition?
Yet Brutus says he was ambitious;
And sure he is an honorable man.
I speak not to disprove what Brutus spoke,
But here I am to speak what I do know.
You all did love him once, not without cause;
What cause withholds you then to mourn for him?
O judgement! Thou art fled to brutish beasts,
And men have lost their reason. Bear with me;
My heart is in the coffin there with Caesar,
And I must pause till it come back to me.

FIRST PLEBEIAN Methinks there is much reason in his sayings.

SECOND PLEBEIAN If thou consider rightly of the matter,
Caesar has had great wrong.

THIRD PLEBEIAN Has he, masters?
I fear there will a worse come in his place.

other "honorable men." A performance note: As Antony begins to speak and all through his oration, the crowd responds, both as indicated by the author's written lines for the Plebeians and at other places the cast and director find appropriate. No actor can outshout an unrestrained crowd, and many an Antony, trying to do so on the first day of rehearsal, has developed vocal strain which has stayed with him through the run. While retaining a feeling of spontaneity rising to hysteria, the crowd must be so precisely rehearsed that they are never actually speaking at the same time as Antony.

paid the penalty for it

81-95 "He was my friend, faithful and just to me," Antony begins to build his picture of Caesar. The captives and their ransoms, his pity for the poor, his denial of the crown on the Lupercal—these are Antony's building blocks, and after each he reiterates that Brutus is honorable but says Caesar was ambitious. The actor need not invoke irony yet, as he speaks of Brutus. He is simply demonstrating contradictions and asking his audience to think.

public treasury

on the day of the Lupercalia

96-99 Antony here seems to lose his earnest self-control and bursts out with passionate honesty and a plea for their respect and decency. His audience apparently stands shocked into silence.

100-103 He stares at them, appalled by their lack of "reason," and then craves their indulgence, overcome by emotion. As he controls his weeping and "recovers," he gives the onstage audience a chance to digest his words.

104-113 The Plebeians go from "reason in his sayings" to "Caesar has been wronged," to "We may just get somebody worse," to "He wasn't ambitious." Line 110 means "if it turns out that he wasn't ambitious after all, somebody will be made to pay for Caesar's death." At line 111 attention goes back to Antony, and now, by line 113, the Plebeians are hailing him and then getting themselves quiet in order to hear him out. In production, it will be important that this sequence of change in the crowd's attitude be clearly heard, with Shakespeare's lines coming through and not swallowed in general actor enthusiasm.

FOURTH PLEBEIAN Marked ye his words? He would not take the crown;
Therefore 'tis certain he was not ambitious.

FIRST PLEBEIAN If it be found so, some will dear abide it.°

SECOND PLEBEIAN Poor soul, his eyes are red as fire with weeping.

THIRD PLEBEIAN There's not a nobler man in Rome than Antony.

FOURTH PLEBEIAN Now mark him, he begins again to speak.

ANTONY But yesterday, the word of Caesar might
Have stood against the world. Now lies he there,
And none so poor to do° him reverence.
O masters! If I were disposed to stir
Your hearts and minds to mutiny°and rage,
I should do Brutus wrong, and Cassius wrong,
Who, you all know, are honorable men.
I will not do them wrong. I rather choose
To wrong the dead, to wrong myself and you,
Than I will wrong such honorable men.
But here's a parchment with the seal of Caesar;
I found it in his closet°, 'tis his will.
Let but the commons° hear this testament,
Which, pardon me, I do not mean to read,
And they would go and kiss dead Caesar's wounds,
And dip their napkins° in his sacred blood;
Yea, beg a hair of him for memory,
And dying, mention it within their wills,
Bequeathing it as a rich legacy
Unto their issue.

FOURTH PLEBEIAN We'll hear the will; read it, Mark Antony.

ALL The will, the will! We will hear Caesar's will.

ANTONY Have patience gentle friends; I must not read it.
It is not meet° you know how Caesar loved you.
You are not wood, you are not stones, but men;
And being men, hearing the will of Caesar,
It will inflame you, it will make you mad.
'Tis good you know not that you are his heirs,
For if you should, O what would come of it?

pay dearly for it

so mean in rank as to do

disorder, riot

private room, study

commoners

handkerchiefs

proper

114-163 Antony's first words, after they can hear him again, refer to Caesar's body and the spasm of grief from which Antony has just recovered—picking up from where he left off, but certain now he is not talking to "brutish beasts." At "O masters," he again reassures them that he isn't here to make trouble, and still he uses "honorable men" with all earnestness, all sincerity. But at "I rather choose to wrong the dead . . . and you," he comes to the very brink of inciting them. As this precise moment, instead of letting them think too long about what he's said, he produces the parchment— " 'tis his will." By "which pardon me, I do not mean to read," the theatre audience begins visibly to enjoy Antony's devices. If the actor is careful to play everything "straight" and without comment, for after all, Antony's life is in danger if the people realize how they are being played upon, the theatre audience will become increasingly enthralled. The actor's danger is that their chuckles and even laughter may entice him into a too-early sarcasm, which will destroy the belief he has been creating. But, as he talks about "kissing Caesar's wounds" and "sacred blood" and "legacy unto their issue," his fervor must touch the crowd, and his speech can begin to move into the true "rabble rouser's" high gear. Someone shouts the demand that he read the will, and the crowd begins to chant. By now he really "has" them. When he wants them to respond, he asks a question—"oh, what would come of it?" or makes a strong sentence-ending—"I do fear it." And now, when he says "honorable men," still earnestly, his audience picks up his words and supplies the irony: "They were traitors. Honorable men!" From the first mention of the will until line 152, "You will compel me then to read the will?" there has been one long build. Most directors cannot resist the crowd shouting an enormous assent to that question, and why should they—for now comes a shifting of the gears again. There is a solemnity as well as an urgent tension about "Then make a ring about the corpse of Caesar . . ." The crowd urges him on and

FOURTH PLEBEIAN Read the will, we'll hear it, Antony.
You shall read us the will, Caesar's will.

ANTONY Will you be patient? Will you stay awhile?
I have o'ershot myself° to tell you of it.
I fear I wrong the honorable men
Whose daggers have stabbed Caesar; I do fear it.

FOURTH PLEBEIAN They were traitors. Honorable men!

ALL The will! The testament!

SECOND PLEBEIAN They were villains, murderers. The will! Read the will!

ANTONY You will compel me then to read the will?
Then make a ring about the corpse of Caesar,
And let me show you him that made the will.
Shall I descend?° And will you give me leave?

ALL Come down.

SECOND PLEBEIAN Descend.

THIRD PLEBEIAN You shall have leave.

FOURTH PLEBEIAN A ring, stand round.

FIRST PLEBEIAN Stand from the hearse, stand from the body.

SECOND PLEBEIAN Room for Antony, most noble Antony.

ANTONY Nay, press not so upon me; stand far° off.

ALL Stand back! Room! Bear° back!

ANTONY If you have tears, prepare to shed them now.
You all do know this mantle.° I remember
The first time ever Caesar put it on;
'Twas on a summer's evening in his tent,
That day he overcame the Nervii.°
Look, in this place ran Cassius' dagger through.
See what a rent the envious° Casca made.
Through this the well-belovèd Brutus stabbed;
And as he plucked his cursèd steel away,
Mark how the blood of Caesar followed it,
As rushing out of doors to be resolved°

there is an eager but respectful shifting and jostling before the next section of the scene. Antony's "Nay, press not so upon me" is a tiny reminder of Casca's Act I characterization of the mob, and it serves here to remind us, although it musn't be over-pointed for humor, that Antony is indeed orchestrating this whole business. After line 163, with everyone demanding "Stand back," etc., Antony has, as the director Margaret Webster used to say, "earned credit" for a softer, more tender, more emotional tone as he tugs at their heartstrings.

gone further than I intended

i.e., from the "pulpit," or raised platform, from which Antony has been speaking

either "farther" or "far"

move

cloak (the Roman toga)

a fierce Gallic tribe conquered by Caesar in 57 B.C.

malicious

learn for certain

164-192 His first line, "If you have tears..." is just a simple statement, or warning. As he reminds the crowd of the mantle, our audience should remember that some of the onstage audience would have been veterans of Caesar's wars, and everyone there would have seen Caesar, in parades or triumphs, probably wearing this very mantle. In the Elizabethan costume of Shakespeare's own period, it was certainly logical that the cloak we saw Caesar don on his way to the Capitol would have been a cloak he might have worn on a day of battle. When the production elects to use Roman costume, with actors in ceremonial togas, this sequence loses in logic. The usual solution, if Roman costume is wanted, is to have Caesar put on the red Imperial toga, not really in use

If Brutus so unkindly° knocked°, or no;
For Brutus, as you know, was Caesar's angel.°
Judge, O you gods, how dearly Caesar loved him.
This was the most unkindest° cut of all;
For when the noble Caesar saw him stab,
Ingratitude, more strong than traitors' arms,
Quite vanquished him. Then burst his mighty heart;
And in his mantle muffling up his face,
Even at the base° of Pompey's statue,
Which all the while ran blood,° great Caesar fell.
What a fall was there, my countrymen!
Then I, and you, and all of us fell down,
Whilst bloody treason flourished° over us.
O now you weep, and I perceive you feel
The dint° of pity. These are gracious° drops.
Kind souls, what° weep you when you but behold
Our Caesar's vesture° wounded? Look you here,
Here is himself, marred° as you see with° traitors.

FIRST PLEBEIAN O piteous spectacle!

SECOND PLEBEIAN O noble Caesar!

THIRD PLEBEIAN O woeful day!

FOURTH PLEBEIAN O traitors, villains!

FIRST PLEBEIAN O most bloody sight!

SECOND PLEBEIAN We will be revenged.

ALL Revenge! About!° Seek! Burn! Fire! Kill! Slay!
Let not a traitor live!

ANTONY Stay, countrymen,

FIRST PLEBEIAN Peace there! Hear the noble Antony.

SECOND PLEBEIAN We'll hear him, we'll follow him, we'll die with him.

ANTONY Good friends, sweet friends, let me not stir you up
To such a sudden flood of mutiny.
They that have done this deed are honorable.
What private griefs° they have, alas, I know not,
That made them do it. They are wise and honorable,

unnaturally and cruelly rapped on a door/delivered a powerful blow

dearest friend,darling

most unnatural and cruel

pedestal

(according to popular belief, the corpse of a murdered man bleeds in the presence of his murderer)

swaggered

force full of grace, virtuous

why

garment

mangled, ruined by

i.e., let us go about our business

personal grievances

till a later day, which looks at least somewhat military. A duplicate version, with appropirate rents and stains, over a duplicate bloodstained tunic, is then put on the "corpse" for the oration, and Antony, beside the body, demonstrates as the text indicates. This entire section seems to require great simplicity and tenderness of the actor, not releasing his passion until line 187—"Whilst bloody treason flourished over us." People in the crowd are by now weeping openly, on which he comments, and then, lines 191-192, he really lets go, as he violently pulls the mantle away: "Look you here, / Here is himself, marred as you see with traitors."

193-200 Shakespeare's written lines for the crowd graph the transition from grief to rage and mutiny through which the crowd must pass. Remember, these sentiments will be echoed by improvisations throughout the passage. "Burn! Fire! Kill!," etc., suggests a violent rush toward the various exits, from which members of the crowd call the others back.

204-228 The actor playing Antony will still be wise to retain his desperate sincerity throughout these references to the "honorable" men, for at line 210 he must not sound like an "orator" and he must be forcefully credible as a "plain blunt man," though we sophisticates in the theatre audience understand his

And will no doubt with reasons answer you.
I come not, friends, to steal away your hearts;
I am no orator, as Brutus is,
But, as you know me all, a plain blunt man
That love my friend; and that they know full well
That gave me public leave to speak° of him.
For I have neither wit, nor words, nor worth,
Action°, nor utterance°, nor the power of speech
To stir men's blood.° I only speak right on.°
I tell you that which you yourselves do know,
Show you sweet Caesar's wounds, poor poor dumb mouths,
And bid them speak for me. But were I Brutus,
And Brutus Antony, there were an Antony
Would ruffle° up your spirits, and put a tongue
In every wound of Caesar, that should move
The stones of Rome to rise and mutiny.

ALL We'll mutiny.

FIRST PLEBEIAN We'll burn the house of Brutus.

THIRD PLEBEIAN Away, then; come, seek the conspirators.

ANTONY Yet hear me, countrymen; yet hear me speak.

ALL Peace, ho! Hear Antony, most noble Antony.

ANTONY Why, friends, you go to do you know not what.
Wherein hath Caesar thus deserved your loves?
Alas, you know not; I must tell you then.
You have forgot the will I told you of.

ALL Most true, the will; let's stay and hear the will.

ANTONY Here is the will, and under Caesar's seal.
To every Roman citizen he gives,
To every several° man, seventy-five drachmas.°

SECOND PLEBEIAN Most noble Caesar, we'll revenge his death.

THIRD PLEBEIAN O royal° Caesar!

ANTONY Hear me with patience.

ALL Peace, ho!

purpose clearly. In a successful performance this line may well get an audible laugh, but a judicious Antony will drive on, passionate, fervent, and honest, to his ringing exhortation at the end to "rise and mutiny." Once more the crowd stands on the brink, and once more he stops them, with total control. By now they seem to be answering to his slightest cue.

permission to speak in public

the gesture appropriate to an orator good delivery

passions directly

stir to rage

229-255 Antony has one last ploy, designed to bring them to the highest pitch. He challenges them as to what they're up to—and then springs his reminder about "the will." They eagerly attend, and now he is almost a cheerleader, starting and stopping the "mob" as with the push of a button. He whips them up, with all the force at his command, to the great climax, "When comes such another?" and at last releases the forces he has stirred up. The crowd responds with fierce hysteria, and as much violence as the director can muster will serve the production well here. Caesar's body must be lifted up (aloft on shoulders is effective) and borne off in the rush. After they've gone and the noise of the insurrection is somewhat muted by distance, Antony can gloat over what he has accomplished.

individual ancient Greek silver coins

noble, munificent

ANTONY Moreover, he hath left you all his walks,
His private arbors, and new-planted orchards,°
On this side Tiber; he hath left them you,
And to your heirs for ever: common pleasures,°
To walk abroad and recreate yourselves.
Here was a Caesar! When comes such another?

FIRST PLEBEIAN Never, never. Come, away, away!
We'll burn his body in the holy place,
And with the brands fire the traitors' houses.
Take up the body.

SECOND PLEBEIAN Go fetch fire.

THIRD PLEBEIAN Pluck down benches.

FOURTH PLEBEIAN Pluck down forms°, windows°, anything.

Exit PLEBEIANS *[with* CAESAR'S *body].*

ANTONY Now let it work°. Mischief, thou art afoot,
Take thou what course thou wilt.

Enter SERVANT.

How now, fellow?

SERVANT Sir, Octavius is already come to Rome.

ANTONY Where is he?

SERVANT He and Lepidus° are at Caesar's house.

ANTONY And thither will I straight° to visit him.
He comes upon a wish.° Fortune is merry,°
And in this mood will give us anything.

SERVANT I heard him say Brutus and Cassius
Are rid° like madmen through the gates of Rome.

ANTONY Belike° they had some notice of° the people
How I had moved them. Bring me to Octavius. *Exeunt.*

gardens

public pleasure grounds

long benches shutters

i.e., do its work

256-265 The Servant whom we saw earlier enters hurriedly with the news of Octavius' arrival, which Antony seizes with eager energy. The Servant gives Antony the good news of the flight of Brutus and Cassius, and the scene ends with Antony's glint of triumph as he understates his success: "some notice of the people / How I had moved them." But his "Bring me to Octavius" is brisk with business.

(Marcus Aemilius Lepidus became one of the Triumvirate with Antony and Octavius)

straightway, at once

according to my wish i.e., we are favored by the fickle goddess Fortuna

have ridden

probably news about

Scene iii *Enter* CINNA *the Poet, and after him the* PLEBEIANS.

CINNA I dreamt tonight° that I did feast with Caesar,
And things unluckily charge my fantasy.°
I have no will to wander forth° of doors,
Yet something leads me forth.

FIRST PLEBEIAN What is your name?

SECOND PLEBEIAN Whither are you going?

THIRD PLEBEIAN Where do you dwell?

FOURTH PLEBEIAN Are you a married man or a bachelor?

SECOND PLEBEIAN Answer every man directly.°

FIRST PLEBEIAN Ay, and briefly.

FOURTH PLEBEIAN Ay, and wisely.

THIRD PLEBEIAN Ay, and truly, you were best.

CINNA What is my name? Whither am I going? Where do I dwell? Am I a married man or a bachelor? Then, to answer every man directly and briefly, wisely and truly: wisely I say, I am a bachelor.

SECOND PLEBEIAN That's as much as to say, they are fools that marry. You'll bear me a bang° for that, I fear. Proceed directly.

CINNA Directly° I am going to Caesar's funeral.

FIRST PLEBEIAN As a friend or an enemy?

CINNA As a friend.

SECOND PLEBEIAN That matter is answered directly.

FOURTH PLEBEIAN For your dwelling—briefly.

CINNA Briefly, I dwell by the Capitol.

THIRD PLEBEIAN Your name, sir, truly.

CINNA Truly, my name is Cinna.

FIRST PLEBEIAN Tear him to pieces, he's a conspirator.

CINNA I am Cinna the poet, I am Cinna the poet.

Stage Directions In the 19th Century this scene was often cut as anticlimactic. In our less romantic times the scene has regained the stage.

the night just past

my imagination is burdened with thoughts of evil omen

out

1-5 The noise of the rape of the city no doubt continues after Antony's exit. Perhaps before Cinna's entrance there might be some violent incursions of crowds again rushing about, but usually Shakespeare hints to us about that sort of thing if he wants it. Cinna the Poet speaks in aside or soliloquy at first, and it would appear that he is being stalked on his entrance or that the marauders slip on during his speech. At any rate, they surprise him.

straightforwardly

5-12 They seem to surround him, each of the four hurling a question. "Married man or a bachelor" seems to be meant to get a laugh, for the scene depends on the horrid humor of the grotesque. Shakespeare's audience knew all too well about an "underclass" possessed only of the values of the jungle. There is real threat within the next three questions, culminating in the sinister "Truly, you were best."

13-16 Poor Cinna does his best to cope logically with what he's been asked. He has the presence of mind to remember each question and apparently who asked it of him, even the adverbs they used.

get a blow from me

straightforwardly/straight, without any detours/ straightway, immediately

17-25 In the Second Plebeian's line about "fools that marry," we get a clear hint that logic will do Cinna no good, but as the following questions and answers come, the pressure seems to be off. His answers seem to be accepted, and even with some politeness.

26-35 As bad luck would have it, his family name is the same as one of the conspirators, and his blood-maddened captors need only this hint to do what they meant to do anyway. "Tear him for his bad verses," tells the whole story. "Pluck out his heart" can be taken literally by the director, as long as the audience

FOURTH PLEBEIAN Tear him for his bad verses, tear him for his bad verses.

CINNA I am not Cinna the conspirator.

FOURTH PLEBEIAN It is no matter, his name's Cinna; pluck but his name out of his heart, and turn him going.°

THIRD PLEBEIAN Tear him, tear him! Come, brands, ho! firebrands! To Brutus', to Cassius', burn all! Some to Decius' house and some to Casca's; some to Ligarius'. Away, go!

Exeunt all the PLEBEIANS *[with* CINNA*].*

is not so close that the stage trickery is revealed. The real climax of the unthinking violence Caesar's death has unleashed on the society comes with Cinna's murder and the general exit which follows. Again, a film or a stage production of operatic scale is needed to do realistic justice to such a scene, and in today's live theatre other means must be found to give the theatre audience a sense of the chaos the author intended. It seems that Shakespeare's theatre did not provide intermissions; today's audience generally expects them. This is the point at which the play changes, and if the production is to be offered in two parts, this is the point most directors will choose for their one intermission.

send him on his way

ACT IV

Scene i *Enter* ANTONY, OCTAVIUS, *and* LEPIDUS.

ANTONY These many then shall die; their names are pricked.°

OCTAVIUS Your brother° too must die. Consent you, Lepidus?

LEPIDUS I do consent—

OCTAVIUS Prick him down, Antony.

LEPIDUS Upon condition Publius° shall not live,
Who is your sister's son, Mark Antony.

ANTONY He shall not live. Look, with a spot° I damn him.
But, Lepidus, go you to Caesar's house.
Fetch the will hither, and we shall determine
How to cut off some charge° in legacies.

LEPIDUS What, shall I find you here?

OCTAVIUS Or here, or° at the Capitol. *Exit* LEPIDUS.

ANTONY This is a slight unmeritable°man,
Meet° to be sent on errands. Is it fit,
The threefold world divided°, he should stand
One of the three to share it?

OCTAVIUS So you thought him,
And took his voice° who should be pricked to die
In our black sentence° and proscription.°

ANTONY Octavius, I have seen more days° than you;
And though we lay these honors on this man
To ease ourselves of divers sland'rous loads°
He shall but bear them as the ass bears gold,°
To groan and sweat under the business°
Either led or driven as we point the way;
And having brought our treasure where we will,
Then take we down his load, and turn him off,°
Like to the empty° ass, to shake his ears°
And graze in commons.°

checked off

Lucius Aemilius Paullus, the brother of Lepidus

(Antony had no nephew named Publius, but he did consent to the death of his uncle, Lucius Caesar)

mark or dot

reduce expenses

either...or

insignificant and unworthy of regard

fit

i.e., the Roman Empire—Europe, Africa, and Asia—parceled out among the triumvirs.

vote

sentence of death condemnation to death or exile

am older

to lighten ourselves of malicious criticism

(a proverbial distinction between the ignoble means and the noble end)

hard labor

send him packing

unladen proverbial for a useless activity

feed on the public pastureland (a sign of hard times)

Stage Directions Note that, unusual for Shakespeare, there is no indication of place or time of day, except for late in the scene where Lepidus's told to go to "Caesar's house," suggesting that we are in Rome. The subject of the conversations (first, who is to be executed, and second, getting rid of Lepidus) suggest a private place, where they are not apt to be interrupted, and an interior, for the same reason.

1-6 The first three lines suggest two "props:" the list of names and whatever stylus, pen or pencil is used to "prick him down." Two new characters enter, and though the reader knows who they are, the theatre audience sees two anonymous people with Antony. The second line identifies Lepidus, and we may remember that we were just told he came to Rome with Octavius. Or we may not. We cannot be expected to assume who the third person is, but he is clearly in some authority, for he tells Antony to designate Lepidus' brother. There is bargaining here, the brother against Antony's sister's son (not the Publius we met earlier, who was established as an old senator), and we sense that Antony and the other newcomer have something in common which leaves out Lepidus.

7-11 Antony sends Lepidus on an errand, suggesting both that he wants him out of the way and that he is relegating Lepidus to an inferior status. The casualness of Antony's answer, "Or here, or at the Capitol" is almost impolite, and that, along with Antony's earlier and cavalier "with a spot I damn him" hints to us that the Antony we are now meeting is a different man than we may have thought him. We are meeting, not a "playboy," not the passionate revenger of his friend, but a calculating and selfserving politician.

12-40 This impression is immediately confirmed the moment Lepidus is gone and Antony moves to attack him. The as-yet-unidentified young man is cooly surprised at Antony's tactic. Antony calls him by name, as he starts his next line, immediately beginning to patronize Octavius and seize the upper hand. There is an easy humor and a "stick with me, kid" quality about Antony's approach to getting rid of Lepidus which seems to rankle with Octavius, whose "You may do your will, / But he's a tried and valiant soldier" is hardly unqualified and cheerful agreement. Antony seems a bit impatient and very much the older and experienced leader counseling his junior as he compares Lepidus to his horse.

OCTAVIUS You may do your will;
But he's a tried and valiant soldier.

ANTONY So is my horse, Octavius, and for that
I do appoint him store of provender.°
It is a creature that I teach to fight,
To wind,° to stop, to run directly on,
His corporal° motion governed by my spirit.°
And, in some taste,° is Lepidus but so.°
He must be taught, and trained, and bid go forth:
A barren-spirited° fellow; one that feeds
On objects, arts, and imitations,°
Which, out of use and staled° by other men,
Begin his fashion.° Do not talk of him
But as a property.°And now, Octavius,
Listen great things. Brutus and Cassius
Are levying powers.° We must straight make head.°
Therefore let our alliance be combined,
Our best friends made,° our means stretched;°
And let us presently° go sit in council
How covert matters may be best disclosed,°
And open perils surest answerèd.°

OCTAVIUS Let us do so; for we are at the stake,°
And bayed° about with many enemies;
And some that smile have in their hearts, I fear,
Millions of mischiefs.° *Exeunt.*

Scene ii *Drum.° Enter* BRUTUS, LUCILIUS, [LUCIUS,] *and the Army.* TITINIUS *and* PINDARUS *meet them.°*

BRUTUS Stand, ho!

LUCILIUS Give the word,° ho! and stand!

BRUTUS What now, Lucilius, is Cassius near?

LUCILIUS He is at hand, and Pindarus is come
To do you salutation from his master.

provide him with a supply of fodder

turn, wheel

bodily mind, intelligence

measure thus

empty, unoriginal

curious sights, artifices, and other men's fashions

vulgarized

i.e., Lepidus takes up a fashion just when other men are abandoning it

thing to be used

armed forces immediately raise an army

closest allies mustered resources extended

immediately

brought to light

most successfully opposed

i.e., like the bear that is chained to the stake in the sport of bearbaiting

at bay, cornered/barked at by dogs who have us at bay

injuries, harms

i.e., drummers playing off-stage

i.e., Titinius and Pindarus enter at a different door from Brutus and his army

word of command, order

40-51 Antony apparently feels he has dealt enough with the Lepidus subject, either because he is confident it is settled or because to say more would be to acknowledge too overtly the negative "vibes" he is getting from Octavius. He heartily urges that they turn to the important matter of dealing with Brutus and Cassius, and with "sit in council" he implies a sharing and an equality which ought to sit well with the younger man. Octavius agrees, but his last thought: ". . . many enemies, / And some that smile have in their hearts, I fear, / Millions of mischiefs" may indicate that he is suspicious of Antony and will be keeping his eye on him. This last thought sometimes has been played as an aside to the audience, Antony having picked up the "scroll" and departed after "enemies," leaving Octavius to address the audience and then follow. No doubt the content of the line works either spoken to Antony or to the audience after his exit. With this scene we have entered the third phase of the play, a military and political struggle dominated by the "ghost" of the absent Caesar.

Stage Directions For the first time, and for the rest of the play, the action moves out of Rome. For a production on the Elizabethan stage or a modern approximation of it such as the original basic stage at Stratford, Ontario, this presents no problem. The major scenic element of the rest of the play is Brutus' tent, easily portable. After that, the scene is the battlefield. A modern proscenium production offering any enclosure or indication of walls for Rome must at this point allow for clearing to an almost bare stage. This becomes the major design consideration for such a production.

1-37 The staging intended by the author here may be hard for a reader to visualize. Here is one way to

BRUTUS He greets me well.° Your master, Pindarus,
In his own change, or by ill officers,°
Hath given me some worthy° cause to wish
Things done undone; but if he be at hand,
I shall be satisfied.°

PINDARUS I do not doubt
But that my noble master will appear
Such as he is, full of regard and honor.°

BRUTUS He is not doubted. A word, Lucilius,
How he received you. Let me be resolved.°

LUCILIUS With courtesy and with respect enough,
But not with such familiar instances,°
Nor with such free and friendly conference °
As he hath used of old.

BRUTUS Thou hast described
A hot friend cooling. Ever note, Lucilius,
When love begins to sicken and decay
It useth an enforcèd ceremony.°
There are no tricks° in plain and simple faith;
But hollow° men, like horses hot at hand,°
Make gallant show and promise of their mettle;°

Low° march within.

But when they should endure the bloody spur,
They fall° their crests° and like deceitful jades°
Sink in the trial.° Comes his army on?

LUCILIUS They mean this night in Sardis to be quartered.
The greater part, the horse in general,°
Are come with Cassius.

Enter CASSIUS *and his Powers.°*

BRUTUS Hark, he is arrived.
March gently° on to meet him.

CASSIUS Stand, ho!

BRUTUS Stand, ho! Speak the word along.

i.e., he sends his greetings by a worthy means

either because of his own changed feelings or through untrustworthy officers

weighty

receive a full explanation

i.e., respect for you and concern for his own integrity

fully informed

signs of close friendship

conversation

strained ceremoniousness

artifices

insincere very spirited at the start

disposition

i.e., low in sound

let fall, ridges on the necks of horses/part of one's coat of arms nags

fall when put to the test

all the cavalry

military forces

slowly

meet the demands of the scene: Brutus leads his party on from one side. His aide, Lucilius, enters from the other side, bringing Cassius' representative, Pindarus. Brutus commands his escort to "Stand." Lucilius commands Pindarus and his escort to "Stand." Lucilius introduces Pindarus to Brutus and then moves to stand behind Brutus. Brutus confronts Pindarus with his request to meet with Cassius. Pindarus stiffly confirms that Cassius is coming. Brutus moves to beside Lucilius and, aside, sounds him as to Cassius' mood. All this sets up the feeling of unease between the generals which prepares for their upcoming confrontation in the famous "Tent Scene." Drums announcing the approach of Cassius' party are heard ("*Low march within*") and both parties converge at the center, with the commands of "Stand" being delivered and echoed each to his own party.

[FIRST SOLDIER] Stand!

[SECOND SOLDIER] Stand!

[THIRD SOLDIER] Stand!

CASSIUS Most noble brother, you have done me wrong.

BRUTUS Judge me, you gods; wrong I mine enemies?
And if not so, how should I wrong a brother?

CASSIUS Brutus, this sober form° of yours hides wrongs,
And when you do them—

BRUTUS Cassius, be content.°
Speak your griefs° softly; I do know you well.
Before the eyes of both our armies here,
Which should perceive nothing but love from us,
Let us not wrangle. Bid them move away;
Then in my tent, Cassius, enlarge° your griefs,
And I will give you audience.°

CASSIUS Pindarus,
Bid our commanders lead their charges° off
A little from this ground.

BRUTUS Lucius, do you the like; and let no man
Come to our tent till we have done our conference.
Let Lucilius and Titinius guard our door. *Exeunt.*

Scene iii BRUTUS *and* CASSIUS *remain.*

CASSIUS That you have wronged me doth appear in this:
You have condemned and noted° Lucius Pella
For taking bribes here of the Sardians;
Wherein my letters,° praying on his side,°
Because I knew the man, was slighted off.°

BRUTUS You wronged yourself to write in such a case.

CASSIUS In such a time as this it is not meet°
That every nice offence should bear his comment.°

37-53 Cassius is already in full cry as he confronts Brutus with his accusation of unjust treatment. Brutus evenly denies this. When Cassius hotly persists in his accusation, Brutus reproves him for making a scene, and, secure in his own moral superiority, consents to hear Cassius out in the privacy of his tent. Cassius curtly orders his party to stand aside. Brutus does the like, and the generals proceed into the tent.

restrained, austere manner

keep calm

grievances

50-53 *The First Folio* here offers different names for those to whom Brutus issues his commands, and staging would seem to confirm the *Folio*, not later editors. Brutus orders "Lucilius," who has already been introduced and is an officer, to transmit his orders, and tells him to tell "Lucius and Titinius" who need not be on the stage yet, to guard the door. This keeps Lucius off till the next scene. He is a boy, after all, and would be unlikely to order soldiers about. Further, *The First Folio* offers no scene division here, merely saying, "Manent Brutus and Cassius." This suggests that, in production, the portable tent might well have been brought in and set up upstage of the action during the "Stand, stand" flurry of the entrance, and that at the beginning of our Act IV, Sc. iii, Brutus and Cassius, like Caesar going into the Capitol in III, i, simply move upstage as the others go off. Soldiers can even open "wings" of the tent to present an interior rather than an exterior at this time. Various productions have offered this scenic solution, and the text suggests that such may have been the Elizabethan practice.

express freely

listen to you

the troops they command

1-8 Entering the tent, Cassius continues his outraged protest, hotly accusing Brutus of wrongly condemning a person Cassius has supported. Brutus not only does not deny this, but in turn states that Cassius himself has been in error. Cassius, smarting, replies that (to paraphrase) people who need money as badly as we do to pay the troops shouldn't be quite so prudish about how they get it.

publicly disgraced

(generally given in the plural even when a single letter is meant) entreating for him

contemptuously disregarded

proper

that every trivial fault should be subject to criticism

BRUTUS Let me tell you, Cassius, you yourself
Are much condemned to have° an itching palm,°
To sell and mart° your offices for gold
To undeservers.

CASSIUS I, an itching palm?
You know that you are Brutus that speaks this,
Or, by the gods, this speech were else your last.

BRUTUS The name of Cassius honors° this corruption,
And chastisement doth therefore hide his head.

CASSIUS Chastisement?

BRUTUS Remember March, the ides of March remember.
Did not great Julius bleed for justice sake?
What villain touched his body that did stab,
And not for justice?° What, shall one of us,
That struck the foremost man of all this world
But for supporting robbers, shall we now
Contaminate our fingers with base bribes,
And sell the mighty space of our large honors°
For so much trash° as may be graspèd thus?
I had rather be a dog, and bay° the moon,
Than such a Roman.

CASSIUS Brutus, bait° not me,
I'll not endure it. You forget yourself
To hedge me in.° I am a soldier, I,
Older in practice, abler than yourself
To make conditions.°

BRUTUS Go to;° you are not, Cassius.

CASSIUS I am.

BRUTUS I say you are not.

CASSIUS Urge° me no more, I shall forget myself.
Have mind upon your health.° Tempt° me no farther.

BRUTUS Away, slight° man!

CASSIUS Is't possible?

accused of having avid desire for money, esp. bribes

traffic in

9-28 Brutus then proceeds to bulldoze straight through Cassius' fulminations with his righteous argument that Cassius himself has been accused of an "itching palm," and that those who in honor killed Caesar for his corruption must not be guilty themselves. He contemptuously declares himself above such practices. The actor playing Brutus must hold himself in here, for, certain of his own virtue, he doesn't need to raise his voice.

lends its authority to

i.e., who could be such a villain as to stab Caesar for any reason other than the cause of justice

i.e., use our integrity for influence-peddling and the selling of public offices

money

bark at

harass

limit my authority

manage affairs

colloquial exclamation like "come off it"

29-38 Cassius, stung, asserts his greater experience as a soldier as a reason he should be given his head. Brutus, though impatient and sorely tried, still holds himself in and simply dismisses these assertions as nonsense. Cassius, beside himself, blusters out a threat, which Brutus, in disgust, rebuts with "slight man." This truly hurts Cassius, who recoils in disbelief at "I'st possible?" Like a lover's quarrel, this one flares beyond reason because of the unspoken pressures and tensions in the larger situation.

provoke

safety provoke

insignificant

BRUTUS Hear me, for I will speak.
Must I give way and room to your rash choler?°
Shall I be frighted when a madman stares?°

CASSIUS O ye gods, ye gods! Must I endure all this?

BRUTUS All this? Ay, more. Fret till your proud heart break.
Go show your slaves how choleric you are,
And make your bondmen tremble. Must I budge?°
Must I observe° you? Must I stand and crouch°
Under your testy humor?° By the gods,
You shall digest the venom of your spleen°
Though it do split you. For, from this day forth,
I'll use you for my mirth, yea, for my laughter,
When you are waspish.

CASSIUS Is it come to this?

BRUTUS You say you are a better soldier.
Let it appear so; make your vaunting° true,
And it shall please me well. For mine own part,
I shall be glad to learn of° noble men.

CASSIUS You wrong me every way; you wrong me, Brutus.
I said an elder soldier, not a better.
Did I say "better"?

BRUTUS If you did, I care not.

CASSIUS When Caesar lived, he durst not thus have moved° me.

BRUTUS Peace, peace! You durst° not so have tempted° him.

CASSIUS I durst not?

BRUTUS No.

CASSIUS What, durst not tempt him?

BRUTUS For your life you durst not.

CASSIUS Do not presume too much upon my love;
I may do that° I shall be sorry for.

BRUTUS You have done that you should be sorry for.
There is no terror, Cassius, in your threats;
For I am armed so strong in honesty°

give scope and freedom to your explosive temper

glares

flinch

be obsequious to   bow

irritable disposition

swallow in silence the poison of your temper

boasting

hear about the existence of/ take lessons from

angered, exasperated

old past tense of "dare"   provoked

that which

integrity

38-82 Brutus at this point has had all he can take, and the pent-up anger breaks through his effort at reserve. He blasts out at Cassius' propensity to make theatrical scenes and take his anger out on others. He lets him have it for the "better soldier" boast and accuses Cassius of not daring to treat Caesar so. This drives Cassius to make another threat—to "do something he shall be sorry for," and Brutus takes those words up as the beginning of a long, self-righteous tirade which is, essentially, illogical. He sent to Cassius for money, "since he can raise no money by vile means," and Cassius wouldn't let him have it. It is, apparently, Cassius who must "wring from the hard hands of peasants their vile trash by any indirection." In other words, "just send it to me—I don't want to know where it comes from." "Deniability" is the modern word for what Brutus seems to want, but it looks as if he is seeking deniability under accusation from his own conscience.

That they pass by me as the idle wind,
Which I respect not.° I did send to you
For certain sums of gold, which you denied me;
For I can raise no money by vile means.
By heaven, I had rather coin my heart,
And drop my blood for drachmas than to wring
From the hard hands of peasants their vile trash
By any indirection.° I did send
To you for gold to pay my legions,
Which you denied me. Was that done like Cassius?
Should I have answered Caius Cassius so?
When Marcus Brutus grows so covetous
To lock such rascal counters° from his friends
Be ready, gods, with all your thunderbolts;
Dash him to pieces.

CASSIUS I denied you not.

BRUTUS You did.

CASSIUS I did not. He was but a fool
That brought my answer back. Brutus hath rived° my heart.
A friend should bear his friend's infirmities,
But Brutus makes mine greater than they are.

BRUTUS I do not, till you practise them on me.

CASSIUS You love me not.

BRUTUS I do not like your faults.

CASSIUS A friendly eye could never see such faults.

BRUTUS A flatterer's would not, though they do appear
As huge as high Olympus.

CASSIUS Come, Antony, and young Octavius, come;
Revenge yourselves alone° on Cassius,
For Cassius is aweary of the world:
Hated by one he loves, braved° by his brother,
Checked° like a bondman, all his faults observed,
Set in a notebook, learned, and conned by rote°
To cast into my teeth.° O I could weep
My spirit from mine eyes! There is my dagger,
And here my naked breast; within, a heart

pay no attention to

irregular and unjust means

vile and worthless coins

split

83-112 It seems to be Brutus' hurt which gets through to Cassius, not his anger. Cassius blames his messenger and then asks Brutus to indulge his infirmities (faults). Brutus is adamant, though no doubt shaken and guilty for having lost his own temper. Cassius, in despair, makes an emotional appeal, offering his life to Brutus as proof of his devotion. This outburst is overblown in tone, passionate in a very un-Brutus, un-stoic way, but utterly sincere, and all Brutus can do (and here he redeems himself in our eyes) is forgive and accept his friend for what he is.

only

defied

rebuked

memorized

i.e., throw up to me (proverbial)

Dearer than Pluto's mine,° richer than gold.
If that thou be'st a Roman, take it forth.
I, that denied thee gold, will give my heart.
Strike as thou didst at Caesar; for I know,
When thou didst hate him worst, thou lovedst him better
Than ever thou lovedst Cassius.

BRUTUS Sheathe your dagger.
Be angry when you will, it shall have scope.°
Do what you will, dishonor shall be humor.°
O Cassius, you are yokèd with a lamb,
That carries anger as the flint bears fire;°
Who, much enforcèd,° shows a hasty spark,
And straight° is cold again.

CASSIUS Hath Cassius lived
To be but mirth and laughter to his Brutus,
When grief and blood ill-tempered° vexeth him?

BRUTUS When I spoke that, I was ill-tempered too.

CASSIUS Do you confess so much? Give me your hand.

BRUTUS And my heart too.

CASSIUS O Brutus!

BRUTUS What's the matter?

CASSIUS Have not you love enough to bear with me,
When that rash humor° which my mother gave me
Makes me forgetful?

BRUTUS Yes, Cassius, and from henceforth,
When you are over-earnest with your Brutus,
He'll think your mother chides, and leave you so.°

Enter a POET, *[followed by* LUCILIUS, TITINIUS, *and* LUCIUS.*]*

POET Let me go in to see the generals.
There is some grudge° between 'em; 'tis not meet
They be alone.

LUCILIUS You shall not come to them.

POET Nothing but death shall stay me.

Pluto, god of the underworld, ruled over all the riches in mines

i.e., your anger shall be free to express itself

i.e., what would seem dishonorable I shall interpret as a harmless expression of your temperament

the hard and cold flint starts fires

with great effort

immediately

113-122 The rage has washed through each of them. The madness has passed. The reconciliation which now comes is meant to be moving, and it is. Brutus even apologizes too, and Cassius, even more ready to acknowledge feeling, asks and receives forgiveness from Brutus, who is surely equally at fault. Throughout this play, Shakespeare is extraordinarily successful in creating characters who are not "bad guys and good guys" but dimensional human beings.

ill-mixed in the body

choleric or waspish temperament

leave it at that

123-140 And now, hard upon one of Shakespeare's greatest scenes comes a chunk of what is generally agreed to be monumentally bad writing. One wants to say, as the 19th Century critics did when they came across something they didn't like, "This surely wasn't written by Shakespeare!" The interruption of the poet has almost always been omitted in production. The

ill feeling

CASSIUS How now? What's the matter?

POET For shame, you generals! What do you mean?
Love, and be friends, as two such men should be;
For I have seen more years, I'm sure, than ye.

CASSIUS Ha, ha! How vilely doth this cynic° rhyme!

BRUTUS Get you hence, sirrah;° saucy° fellow, hence!

CASSIUS Bear with him, Brutus, 'tis his fashion.

BRUTUS I'll know his humor when he knows his time°
What should the wars do with these jigging° fools?
Companion,° hence!

CASSIUS Away, away, be gone! *Exit* POET.

BRUTUS Lucilius and Titinius, bid the commanders
Prepare to lodge their companies tonight.

CASSIUS And come yourselves, and bring Messala with you
Immediately to us. *[Exeunt* LUCILIUS *and* TITINIUS.*]*

BRUTUS Lucius, a bowl of wine. *[Exit* LUCIUS.*]*

CASSIUS I did not think you could have been so angry.

BRUTUS O Cassius, I am sick of many griefs.

CASSIUS Of your philosophy you make no use,
If you give place° to accidental evils.°

BRUTUS No man bears sorrow better. Portia is dead.

CASSIUS Ha! Portia?

BRUTUS She is dead.

CASSIUS How scaped I killing when I crossed° you so?
O insupportable and touching° loss!
Upon° what sickness?

BRUTUS Impatient of° my absence,
And grief that young Octavius with Mark Antony
Have made themselves so strong; for with her death
That tidings came. With this she fell distract,°
And, her attendants absent, swallowed fire.°

cut is an easy one. After the peacemaking, Brutus sets in motion some military matters on the way toward calling to Lucius, who is offstage, for a bowl of wine.

Cynic philosopher/rude, boorish fellow

fellow insolent

i.e. I'll recognize his eccentricity when he recognizes that there is a proper time for outbursts

writing doggerel

fellow (contemptuous)

141-155 Now, out of Cassius' expression of concern at how angry Brutus was, comes the revelation of what Brutus was suppressing. Brutus reveals the news of Portia's death and that her suicide was brought about as a consequence of Caesar's slaying—Brutus' absence and the growing strength of Antony and Octavius—a further reason for Brutus to seek self-justification. Modern actresses playing Portia have difficulty reconciling the woman we see in Act II with this description of her death. Shakespeare was drawing here on Plutarch, and Portias will be well advised to remember that the characters haven't read the play (or Plutarch) and just play the Act II scene as they find it, without trying to act a program note or a scholarly footnote.

give way chance misfortunes

contradicted

grievous

as a result of

unable to bear

became distraught

hot, burning coals

CASSIUS And died so?

BRUTUS Even so.

CASSIUS O ye immortal gods!

Enter Boy [LUCIUS] with wine and tapers.°

BRUTUS Speak no more of her. Give me a bowl of wine.
In this I bury all unkindness, Cassius. *Drinks.*

CASSIUS My heart is thirsty for that noble pledge.
Fill, Lucius, till the wine o'erswell the cup.
I cannot drink too much of Brutus' love. *[Exit* LUCIUS.*]*

Enter TITINIUS *and* MESSALA.

BRUTUS Come in, Titinius. Welcome, good Messala.
Now sit we close about this taper here,
And call in question° our necessities.

CASSIUS Portia, art thou gone?

BRUTUS No more, I pray you.

MESSALA I have here receivèd letters
That young Octavius and Mark Antony
Come down upon us with a mighty power,°
Bending their expedition° toward Philippi.°

MESSALA Myself have letters of the selfsame tenure°.

BRUTUS With what addition?

MESSALA That by proscription° and bills of outlawry,°
Octavius, Antony, and Lepidus
Have put to death an hundred senators.

BRUTUS Therein our letters do not well agree.
Mine speak of seventy senators that died
By their proscriptions, Cicero being one.

CASSIUS Cicero one?

MESSALA Cicero is dead,

candles (a sign of night)

156-163 The business of pledging each other is manly, touching, and effective. It puts a period to the quarrel scene so that the gears can shift and the play can move on. It also plants the presence of Lucius, so that his inclusion at the end of the scene is prepared for. Note, too, that Shakespeare has defined some furniture for us, in that a table must be present to receive the taper and the wine, and that, when Titinius and Messala enter, Brutus says, "Sit we...," four sitting places are implied. This furniture must come on and off with the tent.

consider

164 Cassius is meant to speak of Portia softly enough not to be heard by the entering officers, who apparently don't hear Brutus as he tells him, "No more."

force, army

directing their rapid march
a city in Macedonia

purport

165-178 Putting the quarrel and his grief behind him, Brutus proceeds briskly to compare news with his captains. None of the news is good. Their enemies are approaching, and back in Rome the triumvirate improved the time by killing off senators who opposed them. The tone through here seems grim but businesslike.

condemnation to death
decrees listing those condemned

And by that order of proscription.
Had you your letters from your wife, my lord?

BRUTUS No, Messala.

MESSALA Nor nothing in your letters writ of her?

BRUTUS Nothing, Messala.

MESSALA That methinks is strange.

BRUTUS Why ask you? Hear you aught of her in yours?

MESSALA No, my lord.

BRUTUS Now as you are a Roman, tell me true.

MESSALA Then like a Roman bear the truth I tell;
For certain she is dead, and by strange manner.

BRUTUS Why, farewell, Portia. We must die, Messala.
With meditating that she must die once,°
I have the patience to endure it now.

MESSALA Even so great men great losses should endure.

CASSIUS I have as much of this in art° as you,
But yet my nature could not bear it so.

BRUTUS Well, to our work alive.° What do you think
Of marching to Philippi presently?°

CASSIUS I do not think it good.

BRUTUS Your reason?

CASSIUS This it is:
'Tis better that the enemy seek us;
So shall he waste his means, weary his soldiers,
Doing himself offence,° whilst we, lying still,
Are full of rest, defence, and nimbleness.

BRUTUS Good reasons must of force° give place to better.
The people 'twixt Philippi and this ground
Do stand but in a forced affection;°
For they have grudged us contribution.
The enemy, marching along by them,
By them shall make a fuller number up,

at some time

i.e., in Stoic theory and principle

i.e., let us now take up the work that we, as living men, have to do

at once

harm

perforce, of necessity

i.e., they favor us only through compulsion

179-193 After the news of Cicero's death, however, the scene changes. Messala carefully inquires whether Brutus has heard from or about Portia, and Brutus denies that he has. Why? His denial forces Messala (l. 186) to be the bearer of the bad news. Brutus then must pretend not to have heard it before, and this pretence then calls upon him to demonstrate his celebrated stoicism. Is the performance merely to earn Messala's admiration ("Even so great men great losses should endure") and Cassius' as well ("I have as much of this in art as you, / But yet my nature could not bear it so.")? Does Shakespeare want us to think Brutus does this to provide a good example to his followers? It seems not to serve as a device to create audience sympathy for Brutus, since we cannot be pleased to see him pretend or to watch him put Messala through so difficult a moment. Critics have gone on at length discussing why the news of Portia's death is included twice. Well, some critics theorize that in various of the plays, the compilers of *The Folio* included alternate scenes or endings—just printing both or several different versions, tried at various times in performance, in their anthology—in order not to waste any of Shakespeare's precious words. Note that if one cut out this second telling of Portia's death, one could go from: "Messala: Cicero is dead, / And by that order of proscription," to "Brutus: Well, to our work alive," without damaging either the verse or the continuity of thought. Perhaps a cache of Shakespeare's own prompt books will be discovered one day, resolving all such questions forever. Meantime, most productions of the play just soldier on, using both tellings of the news and forcing the actors to make some sense of it.

194-200 Now Brutus moves to military matters and seems, like a good leader, to seek the advice of his commanders. He asks their opinion of what Cassius evidently thinks is a harebrained idea—"marching to Phillipi presently." "I do not think it good," Cassius bluntly replies, and he readily supports his view with what appears to be sound thinking.

201-224 Once more, Brutus brushes off practical good sense to assert his own "better" judgement. Cassius would have disposed of Antony along with Caesar, and he was most certainly against allowing Antony to speak at Caesar's funeral. He allowed himself to be overruled by Brutus both times. Once again Brutus asserts that his is the better way. It is interesting to consider that all of Brutus' high sounding words about the "tide in the affairs of men" simply

Come on refreshed, new added°, and encouraged;
From which advantage shall we cut him off
If at Philippi we do face him there,
These people at our back.

CASSIUS Hear me, good brother.

BRUTUS Under your pardon.° You must note beside
That we have tried the utmost of our friends,
Our legions are brimful, our cause is ripe.
The enemy increaseth every day;
We, at the height, are ready to decline.
There is a tide in the affairs of men,
Which, taken at the flood, leads on to fortune;
Omitted,° all the voyage of their life
Is bound in° shallows and in miseries.
On such a full sea are we now afloat,
And we must take the current when it serves,
Or lose our ventures.°

CASSIUS Then, with your will,° go on. We'll along
Ourselves and meet them at Philippi.

BRUTUS The deep of night is crept upon our talk,
And nature must obey necessity,
Which we will niggard with a little rest.°
There is no more to say?

CASSIUS No more. Good night.
Early tomorrow will we rise, and hence.°

BRUTUS Lucius! *(Enter* LUCIUS.*)* My gown. *[Exit* LUCIUS.*]* Farewell, good Messala.
Good night, Titinius. Noble, noble Cassius,
Good night, and good repose.

CASSIUS O my dear brother,
This was an ill beginning of the night.
Never come such division 'tween our souls;
Let it not, Brutus.

Enter LUCIUS *with the gown.*°

BRUTUS Everything is well.

reinforced

excuse me

missed, neglected

confined by

what we have ventured or hazarded

as you wish it

i.e., we will scant nature by sleeping only very briefly

i.e., go hence, leave

dressing gown

add up to a justification for Brutus' loss of patience and his willingness to put all his money on one throw of the dice. One could say that with Portia's death and the decline of their fortunes, the conviction has come upon Brutus, though he never admits it aloud, that their killing of Caesar was wrong, and he is eager to face whatever fate awaits him. Perhaps Cassius even senses this and accepts, in yielding to Brutus this last time, that all Brutus has left in him is one final effort. These are questions actors must resolve, and no answer they come up with is wrong, unless it is specifically contradicted by the text.

215-237 Well pleased to have his decision supported, Brutus breaks off the meeting, but, sensing Cassius' disquiet, he asks, "There is no more to say?" Cassius puts a good face on things, and confirms their decision. The farewells to the officers are warm and courteous. Once again Cassius regrets their quarrel, but Brutus reassures him, and the men depart.

CASSIUS Good night, my lord.

BRUTUS Good night, good brother.

TITINIUS, MESSALA Good night, Lord Brutus.

BRUTUS Farewell every one.

*Exeunt [*CASSIUS, TITINIUS, *and* MESSALA.*]*

Give me the gown. Where is thy instrument?°

LUCIUS Here in the tent.

BRUTUS What, thou speak'st drowsily?
Poor knave,° I blame thee not; thou art o'erwatched.°
Call Claudio and some other of my men;
I'll have them sleep on cushions in my tent.

LUCIUS Varrus and Claudio!

Enter VARRUS *and* CLAUDIO.

VARRUS Calls my lord?

BRUTUS I pray you, sirs, lie in my tent and sleep;
It may be I shall raise° you by and by
On business to my brother Cassius.

VARRUS So please you, we will stand and watch your pleasure.°

BRUTUS I will not have it so. Lie down, good sirs.
It may be I shall otherwise bethink me.°
Look, Lucius, here's the book I sought for so;
I put it in the pocket of my gown.

LUCIUS I was sure your lordship did not give it me.

BRUTUS Bear with me, good boy, I am much forgetful.
Canst thou hold up thy heavy eyes awhile,
And touch° thy instrument a strain° or two?

LUCIUS Ay, my lord, an't° please you.

BRUTUS It does, my boy.
I trouble thee too much, but thou art willing.

LUCIUS It is my duty, sir.

(probably a lute)

lad weary from being kept awake so long

rouse

keep awake and attend to your wishes

change my mind

play on tune

if it

238-274 Lucius has entered with the dressing gown and probably at this point helps Brutus to put it on. He apparently yawns as he speaks, for Brutus notices that he is drowsy and asks him to call others to share the burden of standing by in case Brutus requires a messenger. Varrus is quite willing to sit up, but Brutus insists, so they evidently find some cushions and lie down in a corner of the tent. Probably the moment of Brutus finding the book in the pocket of his gown covers any distraction caused by the men getting settled. Then Brutus asks the sleepy but willing Lucius to give him some music, and, at his request, Lucius gets his instrument, lute or lyre, which has also come on with the tent. The song used in the original production has not come down to us, neither words nor music. In Shakespeare's *King Henry the Eighth*, Act III, Sc. i, there is a song which begins, "Orpheus with his lute . . ." which has been often used here, since its text alludes to classical myth, and its closing lines are particularly appropriate to Brutus's condition: "In sweet music is such art / Killing care and grief of heart / Fall asleep, or hearing, die." Lucius falls asleep over his instrument at "This is a sleepy tune," and in a touching moment designed to create the greatest possible contrast with what is coming, Brutus slips the lute or harp out of the boy's arms and puts it aside before he sits to read.

BRUTUS I should not urge thy duty past thy might;
I know young bloods° look for a time of rest.

LUCIUS I have slept, my lord, already.

BRUTUS It was well done, and thou shalt sleep again;
I will not hold thee long. If I do live,
I will be good to thee. *Music, and a song*
This is a sleepy tune. O murd'rous° slumber!
Layest thou thy leaden mace° upon my boy,
That plays thee music? Gentle knave, good night.
I will not do thee so much wrong to wake thee.
If thou dost nod, thou break'st thy instrument;
I'll take it from thee; and, good boy, good night.
Let me see, let me see. Is not the leaf turned down
Where I left reading? Here it is, I think.

Enter the GHOST OF CAESAR.

How ill this taper burns.° Ha! who comes here?
I think it is the weakness of mine eyes
That shapes this monstrous apparition.
It comes upon° me. Art thou any thing?
Art thou some god, some angel, or some devil,
That mak'st my blood cold and my hair to stare?°
Speak to me what thou art.

GHOST Thy evil spirit, Brutus.

BRUTUS Why com'st thou?

GHOST To tell thee thou shalt see me at Philippi.

BRUTUS Well; then I shall see thee again?

GHOST Ay, at Philippi.

BRUTUS Why, I will see thee at Philippi then. *[Exit* GHOST.*]*
Now I have taken heart thou vanishest.
Ill spirit, I would hold more talk with thee.
Boy! Lucius! Varrus! Claudio! Sirs, awake!
Claudio!

LUCIUS The strings, my lord, are false°.

youthful constitutions

i.e., because sleep is an image of death

heavy staff of office

(according to popular belief, candles become dim or burn blue when a ghost is near)

toward

stand on end

275-285 Shakespeare's plays at the Globe were played in daylight, and the only way that light could be thought to dim on cue would be if the actor played that he was having trouble seeing. As atmospheric stage lighting progressed from oil to gas to electricity, so the execution of Shakespeare's "ghost" effects became more elaborate. We should free ourselves from the necessity for illusion to create these Shakespeare ghosts, however, because their real effectiveness comes from the walking and talking appearance, "in his habit as he lived," of someone the characters know is dead. It is Brutus's reaction which gives Caesar's ghost its effectiveness, both his first terror and his subsequent bravery.

286-308 After the ghost vanishes, Brutus calls after it to no avail. He then turns to the sleepers, who have been silent throughout the vision. He tries unsuccessfully to wake them, until finally Lucius mutters that the strings are false. As they come fully awake Brutus asks each of them why he cried out in his sleep. One gathers from this that at some point, probably when the ghost appears and/or disappears, the

out of tune

BRUTUS He thinks he still is at his instrument.
Lucius, awake!

LUCIUS My lord?

BRUTUS Didst thou dream, Lucius, that thou so criedst out?

LUCIUS My lord, I do not know that I did cry.

BRUTUS Yes, that thou didst. Didst thou see anything?

LUCIUS Nothing, my lord.

BRUTUS Sleep again, Lucius. Sirrah Claudio!
[To VARRUS*]* Fellow thou, awake!

VARRUS My lord.

CLAUDIO My lord.

BRUTUS Why did you so cry out, sirs, in your sleep?

BOTH Did we, my lord?

BRUTUS Ay. Saw you anything?

VARRUS No, my lord, I saw nothing.

CLAUDIO Nor I, my lord.

BRUTUS Go and commend me to° my brother Cassius.
Bid him set on his powers betimes before,°
And we will follow.

BOTH It shall be done, my lord. *Exeunt.*

sleepers must "cry out." All three of them deny seeing anything, and it is consistent with other Shakespearean ghosts that the ghost can manifest himself selectively to only those by whom he wishes to be seen or heard. Brutus determines to lose no more time, sending Varrus and Claudio both immediately to Cassius to get the army moving.

pay my respects to

advance with his army early in the morning before me

ACT V

Scene i *Enter* Octavius, Antony, *and their Army.*

Octavius Now, Antony, our hopes are answerèd.
You said the enemy would not come down,
But keep the hills and upper regions.
It proves not so. Their battles° are at hand;
They mean to warn° us at Philippi here,
Answering before we do demand of them.°

Antony Tut, I am in their bosoms,° and I know
Wherefore they do it. They could be content
To visit other places,° and come down
With fearful° bravery,° thinking by this face
To fasten in our thoughts° that they have courage;
But 'tis not so.

Enter a Messenger.

Messenger Prepare you, generals;
The enemy comes on in gallant° show.
Their bloody sign° of battle is hung out,
And something to be done immediately.

Antony Octavius, lead your battle° softly° on
Upon the left hand of the even° field.

Octavius Upon the right hand I; keep thou the left.

Antony Why do you cross me in this exigent?°

Octavius I do not cross you; but I will do so. *March.*

Drum. Enter Brutus, Cassius, *and their Army;*
*[*Lucilius, Titinius, Messala, *and others].*

Brutus They stand, and would have parley.

Cassius Stand fast, Titinius; we must out and talk.

Octavius Mark Antony, shall we give sign of battle?

Stage Directions Whatever tent, table, sitting places, taper, musical instruments, etc., the production may employ must be removed here. In addition, any production will have to address the question of when Brutus gets out of any armor he may wear (before the dressing gown goes on) and when he gets back into it (before entering in this scene at l. 21). No doubt "and their army" will involve two or three officers and a few standard bearers, conveying the sense that the body of "the army" is waiting offstage.

armies

challenge to a fight

1-20 Immediately the rift between Octavius and Antony is made apparent by the "you said they wouldn't but they did" tone of Octavius' first speech. Antony responds in the patronizing manner he adopted with Octavius when advising the dismissal of Lepidus. Of course both of them are pleased that Brutus and Cassius have done the unexpected and unwise thing. The Messenger enters, announcing the approach of "the enemy in gallant show." Antony, as senior commander, immediately assigns Octavius to the left wing of their army. Octavius refuses, demanding the "right." Antony instantly accuses him of "crossing him," and though Octavius denies this, he is adamant about his intention. Their rivalry is made clear.

appearing to oppose us before we call them to combat

aware of their secrets

they would prefer to be elsewhere

inspiring fear in others/full of fear themselves splendid outward show/bravado

persuade us

splendid in appearance/chivalrously brave

red flag

army slowly

level

thwart me at this critical moment

21-65 Brutus and Cassius, with Lucilius, Titinius, Messala, and probably Pindarus and some standard bearers enter on the side of the stage opposite to Antony, Octavius, and their party. Brutus and Cassius confer, Antony and Octavius do likewise. Octavius' line, "Stir not..." is addressed to the men behind him, not to Antony, and it seems that only

ANTONY No, Caesar, we will answer on their charge.°
Make forth;° the generals would have some words.

OCTAVIUS Stir not until the signal.

BRUTUS Words before blows. Is it so, countrymen?

OCTAVIUS Not that we love words better, as you do.

BRUTUS Good words are better than bad strokes°, Octavius.

ANTONY In your bad strokes, Brutus, you give good words;
Witness the hole you made in Caesar's heart,
Crying, "Long live! Hail, Caesar!"

CASSIUS Antony,
The posture of your blows° are yet unknown;
But for your words, they rob the Hybla° bees,
And leave them honeyless.

ANTONY Not stingless too.

BRUTUS O yes, and soundless too;
For you have stol'n their buzzing, Antony,
And very wisely threat before you sting.

ANTONY Villains, you did not so when your vile daggers
Hacked one another in the sides of Caesar.
You showed your teeth° like apes, and fawned like hounds,
And bowed like bondmen,° kissing Caesar's feet;
Whilst damnèd Casca, like a cur, behind
Struck Caesar on the neck. O you flatterers!

CASSIUS Flatterers? Now, Brutus, thank yourself;
This tongue had not offended so today
If Cassius might have ruled°.

OCTAVIUS Come, come, the cause°. If arguing make us sweat,
The proof° of it will turn to redder drops.
Look, I draw a sword against conspirators;
When think you that the sword goes up° again?
Never till Caesar's three and thirty° wounds
Be well avenged, or till another Caesar°
Have added slaughter to the sword of traitors.°

meet their attack when they make it

go forward

blows

i.e., the kind of blows you are able to strike

a Sicilian mountain famous for its honey

grinned

slaves

had his way (in advising that Antony be killed)

i.e., let us return to the business we have in hand

practical trial/logical demonstration

will be sheathed

(all ancient authorities agree on 23)

i.e., Octavius

i.e., in killing Octavius the traitorous conspirators will add another murder to their swords.

after that line do the two sets of generals move center to confront one another. Brutus addresses his enemies formally but courteously, Octavius replies with an insult, which Brutus still meets with courtesy, though his remark is a rebuke. Antony chooses to show his feelings as he accuses Brutus of treachery. Cassius' reply to Antony about the "sweetness" of his words is ironic, for Antony has been anything but sweet. There may be, too, a reference to Antony's double-tongued oration. At any rate, Cassius means to say, "You're a big talker." Antony returns his jibe, which Brutus this time takes up, calling Antony a bluffer. Antony "takes off the gloves" and bitterly blasts Brutus and Cassius as traitors and assassins. Cassius sharply reminds Brutus (and Antony) that if he had had his way, Antony would be dead. Octavius interrupts this slanging match with a vow to revenge Caesar or die himself at the hands of traitors. Brutus bristles at this, there are a few more insults traded, and Octavius leaves, challenging them to "come out and fight," followed by Antony and his party. In this parley, Octavius emerges seeming more heir to Caesar than Antony, partly by having the last word.

BRUTUS Caesar, thou canst not die by traitors' hands,
Unless thou bring'st them with thee.

OCTAVIUS So I hope.
I was not born to die on Brutus' sword.

BRUTUS O if thou wert the noblest of thy strain,°
Young man, thou couldst not die more honorable.

CASSIUS A peevish° schoolboy, worthless° of such honor,
Joined with a masker° and a reveler.°

ANTONY Old Cassius still.

OCTAVIUS Come, Antony. Away!
Defiance, traitors, hurl we in your teeth.
If you dare fight today, come to the field;
If not, when you have stomachs.°

Exit OCTAVIUS, ANTONY, *and Army.*

CASSIUS Why, now, blow wind, swell billow, and swim bark.°
The storm is up, and all is on the hazard.°

BRUTUS Ho, Lucilius, hark, a word with you.

LUCILIUS *stands forth.*

LUCILIUS My lord?

*[*BRUTUS *and* LUCILIUS *speak apart.]*

CASSIUS Messala.

MESSALA *stands forth.*

MESSALA What says my general?

CASSIUS Messala,
This is my birthday; as this very day
Was Cassius born. Give me thy hand, Messala.
Be thou my witness that against my will,
As Pompey was,° am I compelled to set°
Upon one battle all our liberties.
You know that I held Epicurus strong,
And his opinion.° Now I change my mind,
And partly credit things that do presage.°

lineage

childish (Octavius was 21)
unworthy

masquerader party-goer

appetite, inclination

ship

at risk (like a stake in a game of chance)

66-90 Cassius' line, "Why, now, blow wind," etc., while not an aside meant to be unheard by others, seems to be spoken to the gods or fate, or "the wind." Brutus takes Lucilius aside on some military matter, which gives Cassius a chance to make clear to Messala, almost asking his forgiveness, that the coming "winner-take-all" battle was not of his choosing. Then he shares with Messala his sense that their cause is fated to lose, citing omens of disaster. Messala urges him not to believe it, and we see Cassius, like Macbeth in the face of possible defeat, pull himself together with the raw courage of the man of action.

(at the battle of Pharsalia in 48 B.C., Pompey was defeated and later murdered) stake

(Epicurus believed in materialism and that the gods were indifferent to human affairs)

forebode

Coming from Sardis, on our former ensign°
Two mighty eagles fell° and there they perched,
Gorging and feeding from our soldiers' hands,
Who to Philippi here consorted° us.
This morning are they fled away and gone,
And in their steads do ravens, crows, and kites°
Fly o'er our heads and downward look on us
As we were sickly prey.° Their shadows seem
A canopy most fatal,° under which
Our army lies, ready to give up the ghost.°

MESSALA Believe not so.

CASSIUS I but believe it partly,
For I am fresh of spirit and resolved
To meet all perils very constantly.°

BRUTUS Even so, Lucilius.

CASSIUS Now, most noble Brutus,
The gods today stand friendly,° that we may,
Lovers° in peace, lead on our days to age.
But since the affairs of men rests still incertain,°
Let's reason with the worst that may befall.°
If we do lose this battle, then is this
The very last time we shall speak together.
What are you then determinèd to do?

BRUTUS Even by the rule of that philosophy°
By which I did blame Cato° for the death
Which he did give himself—I know not how,
But I do find it cowardly and vile,
For fear of what might fall,° so to prevent
The time of life°—arming myself with patience
To stay the providence of some high powers°
That govern us below.

CASSIUS Then, if we lose this battle,
You are contented to be led in triumph°
Thorough the streets of Rome?

BRUTUS No, Cassius, no. Think not, thou noble Roman,
That ever Brutus will go bound to Rome;
He bears too great a mind. But this same day

foremost standard

swooped down

accompanied

(all birds of evil omen that feed on carrion)

i.e., sick and ready to be their prey

foreboding death

die

resolutely

91-124 Brutus has finished his business aside with Lucilius, and the two generals meet at the center. They are solemn, knowing this may well be the last time they'll see each other. Cassius wants to know what Brutus means to do if they lose. Brutus says he means not to commit suicide but to wait for the decision of providence. Cassius incredulously demands, "Would you accept capture?" Brutus assures him he will not. Then, accepting with what seems to be relief that the end of all this is near, he offers Cassius an earnest farewell—without really answering the question Cassius asked about what he'll do in the face of defeat. "Not suicide, not capture?" Death in battle? Cassius, too, says his farewell. Brutus yearns to know how it will end, but with true stoic courage accepts that, as Shakespeare puts it elsewhere, "Time and the hour runs through the roughest day." With "Come, ho! Away!" he signals the start of the final battle.

may the gods today be well-disposed to us

close friends

remain always doubtful

let's think about what we will do if the worst should occur

Stoicism, which considered suicide cowardly

Marcus Cato, who committed suicide to avoid capture by Caesar

befall

anticipate and thus forestall (by suicide) the natural term of life

to await the disposition of whatever exalted forces

as a captive in a victory procession

Must end that work the ides of March begun.
And whether we shall meet again I know not;
Therefore our everlasting farewell take:
For ever and for ever farewell, Cassius.
If we do meet again, why, we shall smile;
If not, why then this parting was well made.

CASSIUS For ever and for ever farewell, Brutus.
If we do meet again, we'll smile indeed;
If not, 'tis true this parting was well made.

BRUTUS Why then, lead on. O that a man might know
The end of this day's business ere it come!
But it sufficeth that the day will end,
And then the end° is known. Come, ho! Away! *Exeunt.*

Scene ii *Alarum.° Enter* BRUTUS *and* MESSALA.

BRUTUS Ride, ride, Messala, ride, and give these bills°
Unto the legions on the other side.° *Loud alarum.*
Let them set on° at once, for I perceive
But cold demeanor° in Octavio's wing,
And sudden push° gives them the overthrow.
Ride, ride, Messala; let them all come down. *Exeunt.*

Scene iii *Alarums. Enter* CASSIUS *and* TITINIUS.

CASSIUS O look, Titinius, look, the villains° fly!
Myself have to mine own turned enemy.
This ensign° here of mine was turning back;
I slew the coward, and did take it° from him.

TITINIUS O Cassius, Brutus gave the word° too early,
Who, having some advantage on Octavius,
Took it too eagerly. His soldiers fell to spoil,°
Whilst we by Antony are all enclosed.

conclusion/issue, result/true purpose

a call to arms played on drums and trumpets

written papers (containing military orders)

the other wing of the army

move forward (to the attack)

lack of fighting spirit

attack

Stage Directions Our modern scene divisions have even less meaning in the battle scenes of this play than elsewhere, since these short segments of action are cinematic in their fluid montage. Brutus and Cassius are meant to be at different locations on the battlefield, but about the only way of showing this on the Elizabethan stage was to have the two groups use separate sides of the stage. Note too that in this first "battle" Shakespeare never shows us any fighting. We see only the self-defeat of Brutus and Cassius.

1-6 This "scene," one speech long, gives us Brutus seizing what he thinks is an opportunity for victory. He is on fire with hope.

i.e., his own cowardly troops

standard-bearer

i.e., the standard

order

looting

1-8 In "another part of the field," Shakespeare gives us an immediate reversal of fortunes, as Cassius tells us of taking the battle flag he enters with from a fleeing soldier and killing the coward. Titinius explains why Brutus' precipitate move against Octavius gave Antony a chance to encircle them.
Line 9 through line 19: Pindarus rushes in, confirming the presence of Antony's forces at their rear. Cassius sees that his tents are indeed in flames, although he refuses to retreat further than the "hill" he is on. Cassius, from his vantage point, sees a body of troops approaching and sends Titinius to ascertain their identity. Note how Shakespeare carefully keeps Titinius' horse offstage.

Enter PINDARUS.

PINDARUS Fly further off, my lord, fly further off;
Mark Antony is in your tents, my lord.
Fly, therefore, noble Cassius, fly far° off.

CASSIUS This hill is far enough. Look, look, Titinius.
Are those my tents where I perceive the fire?

TITINIUS They are, my lord.

CASSIUS Titinius, if thou lovest me,
Mount thou my horse, and hide thy spurs in him
Till he have brought thee up to yonder troops
And here again, that I may rest assured
Whether yond troops are friend or enemy.

TITINIUS I will be here again even with a thought.° *Exit.*

CASSIUS Go, Pindarus, get higher on that hill;
My sight was ever thick.° Regard° Titinius,
And tell me what thou not'st about the field.

[*Exit* PINDARUS.]

This day I breathèd first: time is come round,
And where I did begin, there shall I end;
My life is run his compass.° Sirrah, what news?

PINDARUS (*Above.*°) O my lord!

CASSIUS What news?

PINDARUS Titinius is enclosèd round about
With horsemen that make to him on the spur; °
Yet he spurs on. Now they are almost on him.
Now, Titinius! Now some light.° O he lights too!
He's ta'en. (*Shout.*) And hark, they shout for joy.

CASSIUS Come down; behold no more.
O coward that I am to live so long
To see my best friend ta'en before my face.

Enter PINDARUS.

either "farther" or "far"

i.e., with the speed of thought

dim, myopic   observe

20 35 The device of Cassius' sight being "ever thick" justifies Pindarus' blow-by-blow account from "higher on that hill." Pindarus apparently exits to get to the "inner above." We have no evidence of onstage access from forestage to upper stage in the Elizabethan theatre. Cassius uses Pindarus' travel time for his short soliloquy, and we can tell by the ten seconds it takes to speak it approximately how far Pindarus had to go. From the upper stage he reports on what he sees. He misinterprets everything. Even by Shakespeare's day uniformity of military garb had not been adopted, and here we have Roman fighting Roman. Pindarus sees Titinius surrounded by a group of horsemen. He dismounts, and they cheer. Pindarus, who has just reported that they are "enclosed" by the enemy, assumes Titinius has been captured. Cassius tells him to "come down," and once more, as Pindarus obeys, Cassius has a short soliloquy.

has completed its full circuit

on the upper stage

approach him at full speed

alight

Come hither, sirrah.
In Parthia did I take thee prisoner;
And then I swore thee,° saving° of thy life,
That whatsoever I did bid thee do,
Thou shouldst attempt it. Come now, keep thine oath;
Now be a freeman, and with this good sword
That ran through Caesar's bowels°, search° this bosom.
Stand not to answer°. Here, take thou the hilts;
And when my face is covered, as 'tis now,
Guide thou the sword.—Caesar, thou art revenged,
Even with the sword that killed thee. *[Dies.]*

PINDARUS So, I am free; yet would not so have been,
Durst° I have done my will. O Cassius!
Far from this country Pindarus shall run,
Where never Roman shall take note of him. *[Exit.]*

Enter TITINIUS *and* MESSALA.

MESSALA It is but change° Titinius; for Octavius
Is overthrown by noble Brutus' power,
As Cassius' legions are by Antony.

TITINIUS These tidings will well comfort Cassius.

MESSALA Where did you leave him?

TITINIUS All disconsolate,
With Pindarus his bondman, on this hill.

MESSALA Is not that he that lies upon the ground?

TITINIUS He lies not like the living. O my heart!

MESSALA Is not that he?

TITINIUS No, this was he, Messala,
But Cassius is no more. O setting sun,
As in thy red rays thou dost sink to night,
So in his red blood Cassius' day is set.
The sun of Rome is set. Our day is gone;
Clouds, dews,° and dangers come; our deeds are done.
Mistrust of my success° hath done this deed.

36-50 Cassius lets us know, for the first time, that Pindarus is a slave and makes the price of his freedom the carrying out of Cassius' death. Shakespeare gives us complete stage directions within Cassius' speech for how this death is to be handled. Cassius offers Pindarus the sword. Pindarus starts to protest. Cassius insists that he take the sword. Cassius covers his face, probably with his cloak but possibly with the battle flag if he still holds it, and at "Guide thou the sword," Pindarus does so. The cloak or flag conceals from the audience where the sword penetrates. One staging problem these lines do not anticipate is the disposition of whatever armor Cassius is wearing. Each production must contend with that in its own way. With his dying breath, Cassius calls out to Caesar, and in that sense, Caesar's ghost is certainly at Philippi. Pindarus, having attained his freedom at what seems to him too high a price, grieves over Cassius' body, and then slips away, hoping to put much distance between himself and all Romans. Thus Shakespeare avoids any encounter between him and the entering Titinius and Messala—who of course come in from one side shortly after Pindarus has gone off on the other.

made you swear when I spared

the inside of the body probe

i.e., do not delay by attempting to answer

old past tense of "dare"

51-71 Messala and Titinius enter, still trading news. The news is not all bad, for the armies are still evenly matched, as Messala suggests, Brutus having defeated Octavius just as Antony has defeated Cassius. They expect to find Cassius to hearten him with their tidings, but see his corpse instead. Titinius goes to the body, for the lines indicate that he is the one who confirms the death. Messala and Titinius both agree, in their speeches over the body, that "mistrust of good success" has been responsible for the "error." This is a fascinating piece of psychology—that a predisposition toward defeat can make one misinterpret the facts. Note that neither Messala nor Titinius talk about fate or portents—or about Caesar, for that matter.

an exchange

a product of the unwholesome night air

anxiety about the outcome of my mission

MESSALA Mistrust of good success hath done this deed.
O hateful Error, Melancholy's child,
Why dost thou show to the apt° thoughts of men
The things that are not? O Error, soon conceived,
Thou never com'st unto a happy birth,
But kill'st the mother° that engend'red thee.

TITINIUS What, Pindarus! Where art thou, Pindarus?

MESSALA Seek him, Titinius, whilst I go to meet
The noble Brutus, thrusting this report
Into his ears. I may say thrusting it;
For piercing steel and darts envenomèd
Shall be as welcome to the ears of Brutus
As tidings of this sight.

TITINIUS Hie° you, Messala,
And I will seek for Pindarus the while. *[Exit* MESSALA.*]*
Why didst thou send me forth, brave° Cassius?
Did I not meet thy friends, and did not they
Put on my brow this wreath of victory,
And bid me give it thee? Didst thou not hear their shouts?
Alas, though hast misconstrued° everything.
But hold thee,° take this garland on thy brow;
Thy Brutus bid me give it thee, and I
Will do his bidding. Brutus, come apace,°
And see how I regarded° Caius Cassius.
By your leave,° gods. This is a Roman's part.°
Come, Cassius' sword, and find Titinius' heart. *Dies.*

Alarum. Enter BRUTUS, MESSALA, YOUNG CATO, STRATO, VOLUMNIUS, and LUCILIUS, *[with* LABIO, FLAVIUS, *and others].*

BRUTUS Where, where, Messala, doth his body lie?

MESSALA Lo, yonder, and Titinius mourning it.

BRUTUS Titinius' face is upward.

CATO He is slain.

BRUTUS O Julius Caesar, thou art mighty yet!
Thy spirit walks abroad° and turns our swords
In our own proper° entrails. *Low alarums.*

impressionable

i.e., Melancholy (Cassius), killed by its own progeny (Error)

72-90 Titinius wants to find the missing Pindarus, presumably to learn in more detail what happened. Messala takes on the duty of going to tell Brutus about Cassius, and Titinius takes advantage of his absence to take upon himself the responsibility for Cassius' death. Placing the victory wreath which Brutus had sent upon Cassius' head, Titinius takes Cassius' sword and kills himself.

hasten

noble

misinterpreted

wait a moment

quickly

honored, esteemed

with your permission i.e., suicide is a proper role for a Roman

91-110 It is Brutus who sees the spirit of Caesar in these events, as he and his party enter to find not only Cassius but also Titinius dead. The "*low alarums*" provide both characters and audience with a sense of pressure. The battle is not yet over. Brutus pays his respects to both "the last of all the Romans" and, after ordering that the funeral be elsewhere, "lest it discomfort" them—and this is the place Shakespeare means for the bodies to be cleared—gives his men a stirring call to arms as they leave, "ere night" for "a second fight.

at large

very own (emphatic)

CATO Brave° Titinius!
Look whe'r° he have not crowned dead Cassius.

BRUTUS Are yet two Romans living such as these?
The last of all the Romans, fare thee well.
It is impossible that ever Rome
Should breed thy fellow. Friends, I owe moe° tears
To this dead man than you shall see me pay.
I shall find time, Cassius; I shall find time.
Come, therefore, and to Tharsus send his body.
His funerals shall not be in our camp,
Lest it discomfort us.° Lucilius, come;
And come, young Cato; let us to the field.
Labio and Flavio set our battles on.°
'Tis three a clock; and, Romans, yet ere night
We shall try fortune in a second fight. *Exeunt.*

Scene iv *Alarum. Enter* BRUTUS, MESSALA, [YOUNG] CATO, LUCILIUS, *and* FLAVIUS.

BRUTUS Yet, countrymen, O yet hold up your heads!

[Exit, with MESSALA and FLAVIUS.*]*

CATO What bastard° doth not? Who will go with me?
I will proclaim my name about the field.
I am the son of Marcus Cato,° ho!
A foe to tyrants, and my country's friend.
I am the son of Marcus Cato, ho!

Enter SOLDIERS *and fight.*

LUCILIUS And I am Brutus, Marcus Brutus, I!
Brutus, my country's friend! Know me for Brutus!

*[*YOUNG CATO *is slain.]*

O young and noble Cato, art thou down?
Why, now thou diest as bravely° as Titinius,
And mayst be honored, being Cato's son.

noble

whether

more

dishearten our army

advance with our forces

Stage Directions At last comes a battle scene.

1 Brutus has an "onstage crossover" as part of the battle, leading one group of soldiers while others remain.

i.e., who is of such base blood that he

Brutus' uncle and father-in-law (Young Cato is the brother of Portia, Brutus' wife)

2-8 Young Cato calls out a general challenge and is apparently overwhelmed as he and Lucilius, probably with others, make a "last stand." Lucilius declares himself to be Brutus probably to earn the real Brutus time to get away.

nobly

9-32 Lucilius is surrounded and captured, still declaring himself to be Brutus. Antony enters, recognizes Lucilius, and receives him as an honorable

[FIRST] SOLDIER Yield, or thou diest.

LUCILIUS Only I yield to die.°
There is so much° that thou wilt kill me straight:
Kill Brutus, and be honored in his death.

[FIRST] SOLDIER We must not; a noble prisoner.

Enter ANTONY.

SECOND SOLDIER Room, ho! Tell Antony Brutus is ta'en.

FIRST SOLDIER I'll tell the news. Here comes the general.
Brutus is ta'en, Brutus is ta'en, my lord.

ANTONY Where is he?

LUCILIUS Safe, Antony; Brutus is safe enough.
I dare assure thee that no enemy
Shall ever take alive the noble Brutus.
The gods defend him from so great a shame.
When you do find him, or alive or dead,
He will be found like Brutus, like himself.°

ANTONY This is not Brutus, friend; but, I assure you,
A prize no less in worth. Keep this man safe;
Give him all kindness. I had rather have
Such men my friends than enemies. Go on,
And see whe'r° Brutus be alive or dead;
And bring us word unto Octavius' tent
How every thing is chanced.° *Exeunt.*

Scene v *Enter* BRUTUS, DARDANIUS, CLITUS, STRATO, *and* VOLUMNIUS.

BRUTUS Come, poor remains° of friends, rest on this rock.

CLITUS Statilius showed the torchlight; but, my lord,
He came not back. He is or ta'en or slain.

BRUTUS Sit thee down, Clitus. Slaying is the word;
It is a deed in fashion. Hark thee, Clitus. *[Whispers.]*

captive. It is clear from Antony's "see whe'r Brutus be alive or dead," and his reference to Octavius' tent that mopping up operations have begun.

i.e., I yield only in order to die

i.e., so much inducement (because I am Brutus)

i.e., acting in accord with his noble nature

whether

has happened

wretched remnant

1-3 After Cassius' death Brutus said that "yet ere night" they would engage in a "second fight." Now, with "poor remains of friends" and the mention of "torchlight" we know the battle is lost and that night has come. Brutus has asked them to sit on the rock, they do so, except for Clitus, who is probably the last of the group to arrive and who needs to report to Brutus on the signal from Statilius.

CLITUS What, I, my lord? No, not for all the world.

BRUTUS Peace then, no words.

CLITUS I'll rather kill myself.

BRUTUS Hark thee, Dardanius. *[Whispers.]*

DARDANIUS Shall I do such a deed?

CLITUS O Dardanius!

DARDANIUS O Clitus!

CLITUS What ill request did Brutus make to thee?

DARDANIUS To kill him, Clitus. Look, he meditates.

CLITUS Now is that noble vessel° full of grief,
That it runs over even at his eyes.

BRUTUS Come hither, good Volumnius; list a word.

VOLUMNIUS What says my lord?

BRUTUS Why this, Volumnius.
The ghost of Caesar hath appeared to me
Two several° times by night: at Sardis once,
And this last night here in Philippi fields.
I know my hour is come.

VOLUMNIUS Not so, my lord.

BRUTUS
Nay, I am sure it is, Volumnius.
Thou seest the world, Volumnius, how it goes;°
Our enemies have beat us to the pit.° *Low alarums.*
It is more worthy to leap in ourselves
Than tarry till they push us. Good Volumnius,
Thou know'st that we two went to school together.
Even for that our love of old, I prithee
Hold thou my sword-hilts whilst I run on it.

VOLUMNIUS That's not an office for a friend, my lord. *Alarum still.°*

CLITUS Fly, fly, my lord, there is no tarrying here.

BRUTUS Farewell to you; and you; and you, Volumnius.
Strato, thou hast been all this while asleep.

4-14 Brutus tells Clitus to sit beside him. What he says apparently appalls Clitus. Brutus moves over to Dardanius and whispers to him in the same manner. After Dardanius also replies in the negative, Brutus evidently moves away, for Clitus and Dardanius can speak together without his knowledge, sharing what Brutus asked. They refer to him as meditating and weeping. Actors, take note.

figurative, especially biblical, for a human being

15-29 Then Brutus calls Volumnius over, and this time we hear the conversation. Brutus speaks of the "ghost of Caesar" appearing twice. We knew of the time at Sardis. He says "his hour is come." He told Cassius he would not slay himself, but that appears now to be just one more illusion. The "*low alarums*" keep the pressure of time and danger on the scene, as Brutus asks Volumnius to hold his sword while he runs on it. Volumnius too refuses.

separate

i.e., how things are

a trap for capturing wild animals/the grave/the abyss of destruction

continuously

30-43 New and closer alarums prompt Clitus to urge that they go. Brutus makes his farewells, including Strato, who has been asleep and knows nothing of Brutus' requests to the others. Brutus earns our

Farewell to thee too, Strato. Countrymen,
My heart doth joy that yet in all my life
I found no man but he was true to me.
I shall have glory by this losing day
More than Octavius and Mark Antony
By this vile conquest shall attain unto.
So fare you well at once;° for Brutus' tongue
Hath almost ended his life's history.
Night hangs upon mine eyes; my bones would rest,
That have but laboured to attain this hour.°

Alarum. Cry within, "Fly, fly, fly!"

CLITUS Fly, my lord, fly!

BRUTUS Hence! I will follow.

[Exeunt CLITUS, DARDANIUS, *and* VOLUMNIUS.*]*

I prithee, Strato, stay thou by thy lord.
Thou art a fellow of a good respect;°
Thy life hath had some smatch° of honor in it.
Hold then my sword, and turn away thy face,
While I do run upon it. Wilt thou, Strato?

STRATO Give me your hand first. Fare you well, my lord.

BRUTUS Farewell, good Strato. *[Runs on his sword.]* Caesar, now be still;°
I killed not thee with half so good a will. *Dies.*

Alarum. Retreat. Enter ANTONY, OCTAVIUS, MESSALA, LUCILIUS, *and the Army.*

OCTAVIUS What man° is that?

MESSALA My master's man. Strato, where is thy master?

STRATO Free from the bondage you are in, Messala.
The conquerors can but make a fire of him;°
For Brutus only overcame himself,
And no man else hath honor by his death.

LUCILIUS So Brutus should be found. I thank thee, Brutus,

respect as he acknowledges that every man he's known has been true to him. Still, though, in his assertion that he "shall have glory by this losing day" he stubbornly clings to that self-righteousness we have seen to be his consuming flaw.

all together

i.e., labored only to attain this hour of death

reputation

smack, taste

44-51 Now the enemy is almost upon them. Brutus sends them on their way, keeping only Strato back. Strato seems to be of a lower social stratum. Brutus went to school with Volumnius, Strato is a "fellow" whose life has had some smatch of honor in it. Messala later refers to him as "my master's man," meaning slave or servant. Strato does his bidding, only asking to clasp his lord's hand. With his last line, Brutus comes as close as he ever does to acknowledging that killing Caesar was a mistake. If the sword is held by a kneeling Strato and Brutus wears a cloak, the thrust can be successfully covered as Brutus runs on the sword. Brutus can say his last line standing, as he clutches Strato's shoulders, and Strato is in a good position to help Brutus's body gracefully to the ground.

i.e., Caesar's ghost now need no longer roam the earth

servant

52-67 Trumpets and drums bring the victors onto the stage. Strato still kneels by Brutus's body, and it works well for him to reveal the body to the group if he rises at "Brutus only overcame himself." Octavius strikes the first note of healing with his "All that served Brutus, I will entertain them," and the honorable resolution of the question of how Brutus died helps to continue the sense of returning order.

can only burn his body, not capture him alive

That thou hast proved Lucilius' saying true.

OCTAVIUS All that served Brutus, I will entertain them.°
Fellow, wilt thou bestow° thy time with me?

STRATO Ay, if Messala will prefer° me to you.

OCTAVIUS Do so, good Messala.

MESSALA How died my master, Strato?

STRATO I held the sword, and he did run on it.

MESSALA Octavius, then take him to follow thee,
That did the latest° service to my master.

ANTONY This was the noblest Roman of them all.
All the conspirators save only he
Did that they did in envy of great Caesar;
He only, in a general honest thought
And common good to all, made one of them.°
His life was gentle,° and the elements°
So mixed in° him that Nature might stand up
And say to all the world, "This was a man!"

OCTAVIUS According to his virtue° let us use° him,
With all respect and rites of burial.
Within my tent his bones tonight shall lie,
Most like a soldier, ordered honorably.°
So call the field° to rest, and let's away
To part° the glories of this happy day. *Exeunt omnes.*°

take them into my service

spend

recommend

last, final

i.e., only Brutus was impelled by honorable purposes and for the public benefit of all Romans

noble (the four humors that make up the human body)

i.e., so well mixed

excellence treat

treated with all appropriate honor

i.e., army in the field of battle

share all

68-81: Antony gives Brutus a fitting and graceful eulogy, and although the audience has seen Brutus's faults clearly enough throughout the play, we cannot but agree with Antony's summation that "This was a man." Octavius, as Caesar's heir and therefore the personage of highest rank remaining in the play, gets the last speech, in accordance with Elizabethan practice. Note that the last word in the speech, before the obligatory final couplet, is "honorably," that word which has been used with so many colors throughout the play. There is no accident, either, in the note of irony faintly sounded by "happy day" spoken over the body of Brutus, flanked by Antony and Octavius, who will shortly be at each other's throats.

TEXTUAL NOTES

The text printed in the 1623 *Folio* is the sole authority, and *Julius Caesar* is probably the most accurately printed play in the collection. For proper names, I have chosen the ironically radical expedient of giving them as they appear in the *Folio.* On the basis of North's translation of Plutarch, we know that Shakespeare should have written Marullus rather than Murellus, Varro and Claudius rather than Varrus and Claudio, and Labeo rather than Labio. I have not corrected factual errors such as Shakespeare's reference to Tharsus rather than Thassos as the burial place of Cassius (V.iii.104) and Caesar's "three and thirty wounds" (V.i.52) rather than three and twenty. I have not regularized the colloquial variants of the proper names Antonius, Octavius, and Flavius, which are sometimes given as Antonio, Octavio, and Flavio. In the following collation, all substantive changes from the *Folio* other than obvious misprints are recorded; the reading of this present edition is followed by that of the *Folio.*

I.i 15 *MURELLUS* Flavius

I.iii 131 *In favor's* Is Favors

II.i 40 *ides* first 213 *eighth* eight

II.ii 24 *did* do 46 *are* hear

Iii.i 39 *law* lane 210 *strucken* stroken

III.ii 215 *wit* writ

IV.ii 34-36 Folio does not indicate the speakers of these lines.
50 *LUCIUS* Lucilius 52 *LUCILIUS* Lucius

IV.iii 179-93 This second revelation of Portia's death conflicts with the earlier account in this scene. It appears to be the original version that was afterwards revised.